MW01000397

Steve Wood

Praise for

LEGACY:
A Father's Handbook for Raising Godly Children

"I am so grateful to Stephen Wood for writing *Legacy: A Father's Handbook for Raising Godly Children*. I found myself repeatedly exclaiming '*Yes!*' as I devoured each page of the practical, time-tested wisdom that Steve shares so effectively in this powerful new book. Whether you're a veteran dad with many years of child-rearing behind you or are brand new to the awesome mystery of Christian fatherhood, you *need* to read this book and apply its principles to your own life. If you do, I can guarantee that your wife and children will quite literally be eternally grateful to you for having done so, and God will bless your family in ways unimaginable."

— **Patrick Madrid,** father of eleven,
author, *Search and Rescue: How to Bring Your Family and Friends Into (or Back Into) the Catholic Church*

"*Legacy* is a tough, uncompromising, and timely handbook that lays out the essentials of how to be a Christian father and husband in today's world."

— **Jim Amsing,** father of ten,
Calgary police officer, police chaplain

"*Legacy* is a reference book, pep talk with depth, and coaching guide all wrapped up in one. All fathers serious about their responsibilities should read it and live it."

— **Dave Durand,** father of six,
author, *Time Management for Catholics*, trainer, speaker

More praise for

LEGACY:
A Father's Handbook for Raising Godly Children

"After reading *Legacy* I can only say, 'Warning to Catholic men: Use of this book has been known to cause radical positive, life changing alterations.' This book is not simply another book on fatherhood with information – it will also cause transformation! Men were made for heroism and this book gave me a baptism of boldness.

I spent many years training in boxing and karate gyms to discipline my body; these days I spend much time before the Blessed Sacrament with the Bible, the Catechism and Steve Wood books and newsletters. He is one of the best spiritual fitness trainers for Catholic men in the world today. This book is a 'weapon of mass instruction' and its insightful array of tips and Catholic wisdom should be adopted by every Catholic father as a way of life.

Responsibility for shaping your children's eternal souls is a powerful motivation to answer God's call to holiness as a father. If every Catholic father would read and implement the faithful, winsome, and charitable principles in this book, we would put divorce courts out of business and empty out our jails.

Legacy is vintage Steve Wood at his finest. I wholeheartedly endorse this book and ask that every Catholic man who is interested in the welfare of his family read *Legacy* in order to leave this world a better place for our children."

— **Jesse Romero**, father of three,
lay evangelist, USA middleweight kickboxing champion,
world police boxing champion, veteran deputy sheriff

LEGACY

A Father's Handbook for Raising Godly Children

LEGACY

A Father's Handbook for Raising Godly Children

Stephen Wood

Family Life Center Publications

ISBN-13: 978-0-9727571-3-3
ISBN-10: 0-9727571-3-9
Library of Congress Catalog Card Number: 2005937405
Book layout and cover design: Lisa Denise Harris
Manufactured in the United States of America

Unless otherwise indicated, Scripture quotations are taken from the Revised Standard Version, Catholic Edition [RSVCE], copyright © 1965 and 1966 by the Division of Christian Education of the National Council of the Churches of Christ in the United States of America. Used by permission.

Acknowledgments

I would like to thank my wife Karen, my daughter Stephanie, Philip Cutajar, and Mike Phillips for all of their advice, proofreading, and helpful suggestions.

Family Life Center Publications
22226 Westchester Blvd.
Port Charlotte, FL 33952
www.familylifecenter.net

Dedicated to

the memory of my father, who took me
hunting, fishing, and to church,
and to the fathers of my grandchildren

CONTENTS

INTRODUCTION

Fathers, Fishing, and Faith

I had just finished telling a group of men about the most memorable week of my boyhood: the week my dad took my brother and me on a fishing trip to a remote region of Quebec, Canada.

A man approached me with a serious look on his face, holding his Bible in front of him with both hands. He said, "Steve, I'd like to show you something that I have not shown any other person, except my wife. I've kept it here in my Bible for the past twenty-five years." I had no idea what I was about to see, but whatever it was I knew that it was one of this man's most precious treasures. Trembling with emotion, he opened his Bible and took out a small piece of white notepaper with just a few sentences of handwriting on it. The note was from his dad, who was serving combat duty in Vietnam.

Remember that Vietnam was our first "television war," where bloody casualties were broadcast into our homes every evening at dinner time. It's not too hard to imagine the silent fears of this soldier's son, seeing the nightly news and asking himself, "Will Dad be killed?"

The soldier's twenty-five year-old note went like this: "Son, when I get home from here – and I will – I'm going to take you and your brother fishing. Love, Dad." Fighting back tears, this man told me that his dad did make it home from Vietnam … and that he took his brother and him fishing.

We didn't say too much to each other after I read his dad's note. We just stood there in quiet acknowledgement. We had both grasped the truth that fatherhood was about something much more than going fishing with your sons. We knew that it was really about something so big, so deep, and so profound that words didn't seem adequate to express it.

I think that I'm a fool for trying to put into words what this special "something" is, but since it is so essential to good fathering, I'm going to try.

The exceptional "something" in the connection between dads and their children is really a "Someone." Here is a big hint for all of us: for twenty-five years this man kept his dad's "promise to go fishing" note in the middle of his Bible. He was an average guy, not a theologian or an unusually religious man, but he was certain that the big "something" between himself and his dad had to do with God. He had instinctively discovered that earthly fatherhood is connected to divine fatherhood.

God the Father is the one who makes your fatherhood and mine so important in our children's lives. St. Paul said that earthly fatherhood derives its very name from God the Father (Ephesians 3:14-15). Every child that God sends into the world comes with an intense, built-in yearning for a union with God the Father. All of us, adults and children, are hard-wired for this union with our Heavenly Father. We are all moved in the deepest part of ourselves to find Him. Some of us go on detours (like the excessive pursuit of money, pleasures, pastimes, or addictions) in finding this fulfillment, but we are all driven by it.

In the divine plan, a dad is a vital link in the process of a child finding a sacred relationship with God the Father. Every dad – for better or for worse – is like a living icon of God the Father for his children. Especially in early childhood, a father's daily life in the family (or absence from the family) forms an image of God the Father in his children. This is truly an awesome responsibility for dads.

In case you're panicking as you read this, let me emphasize that you don't have to be a perfect father in order to be a good Christian dad. You and I will never be perfect fathers. There is only one perfect Father, and He is in heaven. Our job is to make an earnest effort to project a decent image of God's fatherhood to our children, with the constant realization that, despite our greatest intentions, our efforts will fall short. That's okay. God's gracious plan includes using our imperfect fatherhood to reflect His image to our kids.

So you'll know where I'm coming from, let me tell you a little bit about myself. I'm the father of eight children, and I've been a dad for the past twenty-five years. I started thinking seriously about fatherhood thirty years ago, while I was a single man serving as a youth minister. I witnessed firsthand both the advantages and the handicaps teens carried as a result of their relationships with their dads. What I learned from youth ministry caused me to take my own fatherhood seriously. I regard fatherhood as one of the most important things I'll do with my life.

For me, fatherhood hasn't been a hobby or a pastime that just gets squeezed in after my career. Fatherhood is God's calling in my life, an essential part of my vocation as a Christian husband. Trying to be a good dad building a legacy of faith, despite my shortcomings, is central to my life's purpose. Please know that I don't claim to have perfect children, and I certainly don't claim to be a perfect father.

Also be advised that I'm not a professional psychologist. Yes, I've studied psychology and counseling, and have profited from it, but I'm not impressed with the majority of psychologists. I realize that some parents are prone to take the advice of psychological "experts" as though it was divine revelation. Quite frankly, it gives me considerable pause if someone claims to be a parenting expert because of his or her psychology or social work degree. Many Christian psychologists have drunk too deeply from Freud's well, allowing the Scriptures and the Church Fathers to take a secondary place in their thinking.

Since I'm not a psychologist or an expert with an infallible plan for fathers, you should be able to relax a bit. I'm just a regular guy trying my best to be a good dad. Therefore, you shouldn't regard the twelve chapters in this book as "The Twelve Commandments for Fathering." It's a mistake to let your anxieties cause you to latch onto any book claiming to have the perfect parental blueprint. Just take the useful things you find in this book and combine them with the good things from your own family experience. If you actually do this, you'll be well on your way to becoming a successful dad.

I've discovered a great irony in fatherhood. Being a dad requires lots of time, sacrifice, and patience. In return, your kids drain your bank account, break your stuff, leave your tools out to rust – and yet you still end up feeling that fatherhood is the most fulfilling part of your life. Yes, fatherhood requires immense self-giving, but isn't that how Jesus told us that self-fulfillment would take place? Despite being a tough and demanding job, the rewards of fatherhood are worth it. Alongside the challenges, I've found fatherhood to be immensely fulfilling – and one heck of a lot of fun. Doing almost anything with your children can make the experience twice as much fun. For example, it's exciting to catch a big fish, but it's exhilarating to see one of your children catch one.

President Teddy Roosevelt, father of six, experienced what I'm talking about:

> There are many kinds of success in life worth having. It's exceedingly interesting and attractive to be … a President, or a ranchman, or the colonel of a fighting regiment, or kill grizzly bears and lions. But … a household of children … certainly makes all other forms of success and achievement lose their importance by comparison.[1]

If you desire a life of true manly adventure, then fatherhood should be your focus. The chapters ahead are designed to equip and encourage you for the most important job a man can have – being a dad.

CHAPTER ONE

A Job for Fathers

During a visit to the magazine section of a mega-bookstore, I looked for *Parents* magazine. I found it in the women's section, right next to *Pregnancy*. Inside *Parents* were ads for women's beauty and sanitary products, along with minivan ads showing moms transporting kids. It was obvious that *Parents* magazine was intended for mothers and not fathers.

If mothers were the target market for just one particular parenting magazine, this would be of little consequence. Unfortunately, *Parents* magazine reflects the concept embraced by our entire culture: parenting is the domain of mothers, to the near exclusion of fathers.

Even Christian circles don't seem immune from this one-sided view of parenting. Women buy the vast majority of Christian family, marriage, and child-rearing books. I remember reading a "Help Wanted" ad for a large Christian family organization seeking an announcer: it said that any candidate must have the skills necessary to relate to women. Nothing was said about a necessary ability to relate to men. Are men optional for Christian family life?

There has been a dramatic shift in American fatherhood and family life that most people are completely unaware of. David Blankenhorn in *Fatherless America* summarizes this change by saying, "Over the past two hundred years, fathers have gradually moved from the center to the periphery of family life."[2]

In eighteenth century America, child-rearing manuals and articles on child discipline were generally written by men for men. Blankenhorn recounts that fathers helped guide the marital choices of their children, guided them into the working world and, most importantly, assumed primary responsibility for their religious and moral training.

What caused such a dramatic shift in American fatherhood? Blankenhorn highlights many of the various causes at work during this period, including industrialization, which separated a father's work life from his home life. There were also important religious dynamics, along with economic causes, which marginalized the father's role.

Starting in the late eighteenth century, American Protestantism was radically influenced by a phenomenon known as revivalism. Revivalism brought a more affective, "feelings-based" approach to Christianity, with an emphasis on the heart, in contrast to the head. The revivalists promoted the ideal of intense religious feelings, which further sentimentalized American Christianity. The revivalist preachers and their increasingly emotional revivals were especially attractive to women.

During this same period, American clergy became increasingly feminized. Historians note that "softer" men were finding their way into the pulpit (a phenomenon that lingers). Their appeals were focused on women-led voluntary associations, and on reform movements like the temperance movement. Men abandoned church leadership as more and more activities were taken over by women. Ministers began preaching that mothers were more important than fathers in child-rearing, in sharp contrast to what had been taught by colonial American ministers.

Men increasingly found their meaning and role in their work life, rather than in their home life. As Anthony Guerra, visiting scholar at Harvard University, has correctly stated, "The [nineteenth century] second Awakening was to become the vehicle for raising women to the head of the family ... a veritable reversal of roles within the family was ... the effect of developments in American Christianity."[3] By the twentieth century, if not before, American Catholics were affected by these currents in our predominantly Protestant culture.

So what can be done to recover fatherhood's active role in family life? The hard work of recovering American fatherhood begins by changing one home at a time. It begins when you and I stand up, and once again shoulder our share of family and child-rearing responsibilities.

As Christians, we have more than just a set of abstract principles for restoring the father's role within the family. We have St. Joseph as a model, and we can follow his footsteps. He was the servant leader of his family, always taking the initiative in leading, protecting, and providing for them. His fatherly training of Jesus from boyhood to manhood was the most important job in the world in his day.

The purpose of this book is to help you recover your role as a Christian father by preparing you to assume the primary responsibility for child training and discipline in your home.

St. Paul, in the context of discussing the roles of husband and wife and the duties of children toward both parents, singles out the father for the duty of child training and discipline. He says, "Fathers, do not provoke your children to anger, but bring them up in the discipline and instruction of the LORD" (Ephesians 6:4).

St. Paul isn't saying that fathers have an exclusive role in child training and discipline, but he certainly implies that they have a primary role. In the mother and father team, moms usually excel in nurturing, although they are certainly involved in discipline; similarly, dads should excel in discipline and training, yet need to be involved in nurturing.

Please understand: the recovery I'm advocating isn't a lurch to an opposite extreme, where fathers would assume all of the responsibility of child training. Parenting is for moms *and* dads. I'm advocating that Christian men partner with their wives in this critical task, and stop dumping all responsibility for the children on the wife's shoulders.

I'm sure you've seen this all-too-common sight: A young family is sitting together at Mass. Mom is struggling to care for the newborn while the toddler is acting up, moving all around, and distracting scores of worshippers. Dad sits there unmoved, pretending that he doesn't notice the chaos going on next to him. Now desperate, the wife looks over to her husband for any assistance he might offer. With an expressionless face, he pretends he doesn't notice her glance. If the toddler can be occasionally restrained, it is up to the frantic mom to do it while caring for the newborn at the same time.

Hopefully, the scenario will change after Dad reads and implements what's in this book. Worshippers will notice the nice young family in front of them. While the mother tends to the needs of the newborn, the toddler seated immediately next to his father seems well behaved. (The father has used the training strategies for sitting through Mass described in Chapter 12.) You notice that, just as the toddler is about to lose his self-control, a brief word from his attentive father seems to restore equilibrium. You wonder why every young family can't be like this at Mass. In reality, they can.

Families and children are transformed when Dad takes an active role in child training, and when he becomes a true partner with his wife in parenting their children.

We need to bury the notion that parenting is just a mother's responsibility. Our country, our Church, and our families desperately need fathers to turn their hearts toward their children (Malachi 4:6). Fathers need to resume their vital role within the family.

The key to Christian fatherhood is gaining a vision of the Faith running through the generations of your family. Dad, you must grasp the truth that creating a legacy of faith through the training and discipline of your children is a real man's job. It is *your* job. In fact, it is your most important responsibility on earth, because whatever you do (or fail to do) as a father will have effects for generations – and for eternity.

CHAPTER TWO

Finding Time
for Fathering

In case you don't like reading and don't plan to finish this book, then just read and heed the next sentence. Practice your faith and remain in a state of grace; love your wife and stay married; be a good provider and tithe; and spend lots of time with your children. That's how to be a good Christian man, husband, and dad in a single sentence. Not too complicated.

The famous comedian Woody Allen (*not* a role model for fathers) once quipped, "Eighty percent of success is showing up." There is no escaping the reality that successful fatherhood is directly dependent upon "showing up" – simply being present and available for your kids. For children, love from their fathers is spelled "T-I-M-E." Yet spending adequate time with their children is a stumbling block for many dads.

The suggestion that quality time can adequately replace large quantities of parental time is lunacy. Don't swallow this fatherhood fallacy. By the time you notice all the adolescent consequences stemming from a lack of fathering time, it's too late to turn back the clock.

Children grow up once. You have exactly one opportunity to be a good dad to your young children. You either seize your moments of opportunity by spending adequate time with your children, or you permanently diminish your effectiveness as a parent. There are no second-chance winners in fatherhood.

Parents in America today spend about forty percent less time with their children than parents did just a generation ago.[4] This works out to about ten to twelve fewer hours per week. Surprisingly, the father's time deficit is particularly prevalent in homes with two full-time wage earners. The fathers in dual-earner homes spend about an hour less with their children *each day,* compared to fathers in single-earner households.[5]

Except for the extreme necessity of wartime father absence, there has never been such a profound loss of fatherhood time in recorded history. This loss of parental time almost guarantees trouble in the teen years, when dwindling parental influence can be eclipsed by the peer group and the media.

Your children in their pre-teen and teen years are going to be in a tug-of-war between the values of the peer group and your morals and beliefs. To win this contest, you must take a proactive approach to fathering by building up the bond between you and your children. By spending generous amounts of time with them throughout their childhood, you overcome peer pressure with parent pressure. Successful fathers don't wait for teen problems to explode. Instead, they make the time investments long before they might seem necessary.

Piggy bank fathering

I call the investment of your time in your child's life, "piggy bank" fathering. Each hour playing catch, going on trips, talking, or working together deposits a few pennies in the fatherhood piggy bank. The good news is that you have a decade's head start on your teen's peers to make your deposits. When the pull of the peer group begins, you'll depend on the systematic deposits you have made to your fathering-time piggy bank. As a dad of three children who have already passed through their teens, four in their teens, and one pre-teen, I can assure you that you'll draw on *all* of the deposits you've made.

How much time?

You might be asking yourself, "Okay, just how much time do I need to be spending with my kids?" One thing is certain: you can't just go with the flow and do what most other fathers are doing. A good starting place is to try to make up that forty percent average loss in parental time over the past generation. Remember, this is just a beginning goal. My personal goal is to spend twice as much time as most others are spending in our increasingly fatherless culture.

Stay-at-home dads?

A small percentage of men have taken the exhortations to spend time with their children to unbalanced extremes. Some guys, for a variety of reasons, become stay-at-home dads and let their wives be the primary breadwinners. Unless there is some type of medical reason, a need for temporary training for career advancement, or some other necessity, the stay-at-home non-breadwinner father is a poor model of fatherhood. Remember, it is by observing you as a breadwinner that your children learn to trust in God's provision and pray, "Our Father in Heaven … Give us this day our daily bread." Men adverse to breadwinning should heed these two Scriptures:

> If any one does not provide for his relatives, and especially for his own family, he has disowned the faith and is worse than an unbeliever (1 Timothy 5:8).

> There is wrath and impudence and great disgrace when a wife supports her husband (Sirach 25:22).

Researchers in the Netherlands have found role reversal risks associated with stay-at-home dads. Divorce is significantly more likely within the first decade of a marriage where the traditional sex roles have been reversed during the first five years and the wife is working outside the home more than the husband. Conversely, the more hours the husband works and the fewer hours the wife is employed, the less likely the probability of divorce.[6]

The ultimate way to find time for fathering

The key to time management for fathers isn't using the right planning system, but receiving divinely implanted priorities. Planning systems are helpful in living out your priorities, and I recommend them. Yet you need more than a self-generated priority in order to spend more time with your kids. Living priorities for Christian men aren't born at a life planning seminar in some hotel conference room. Rather, they flow to dads from the heart of God the Father, by the power of the Holy Spirit.

A father's need is to have God the Father implant just a bit of the divine fire of eternal love for His Son into his heart. Once your heart is touched by the Father, you will be a changed man. Dynamic life priorities – that is, priorities that are actually lived out instead of just hoped for – will flow from a changed heart.

The St. Joseph model for fatherhood

St. Joseph is the world's best father. His fatherhood didn't originate from being the biological father of Jesus. He was given the heart of a father through a bountiful infusion of divine fire into his heart. God is willing to do a similar work in your heart. It is wise to ask for St. Joseph's intercession to obtain divine fire for your fatherhood, since he has already experienced what you are seeking.

The divine plan for building a legacy of faith through child training begins with the transformation of fathers. As you receive the heart of a father, child training becomes a profound, deeply-felt response of your children to your divine transformation:

> And he will turn the hearts of fathers to their children and the hearts of children to their fathers (Malachi 4:6).

Prayer for priorities

To receive the divine fire in your heart, you ask for it in prayer. Every time you pray "Thy will be done on earth [in me] as it is in heaven," your prayer can include the intention of having the heart of the Heavenly Father move your will and fill your heart. I can't assure you that answers to prayer will come like a flash of lightning, but they will be answered – provided you aren't blocking your prayer life with an unconfessed grave sin.

I've discovered a few other prayers to be helpful in keeping priorities straight. Across the top of my daily planner, I often write a short prayer from Psalm 90 that says, "Teach us to number our days that we may get a heart of wisdom" (verse 12). Even our own diligent planning can interfere with finding time for fathering, unless God's wisdom is bestowed upon our efforts.

Psalm 39:4 is another good scripture to use in praying for the bestowal of priorities: "LORD, let me know my end, and what is the measure of my days: let me know how fleeting my life is!" This prayer is useful to keep us from procrastination and the wishful thinking that "tomorrow" we will get around to important family needs. We often think that we have decades left to live – until a health scare shocks us out of our complacency and causes us to focus on the truly important priorities. Life goes by very quickly, and the few years we have to train our children pass even quicker.

St. Paul wrote an exhortation we all need when our busy schedules lead us away from family life:

Look carefully then how you walk [i.e., your direction in life, your goals, and your motivations] not as unwise men but as wise, making the most of the time, because the days are evil. Therefore do not be foolish, but understand what the will of the LORD is (Ephesians 5:15-17).

Shortly after this exhortation, St. Paul discusses marriage and fathers training their children – the priorities for wise men.

Career choices & time for fathering

Coupled with the need for divine enlightenment in living out family priorities are practical time-saving strategies that help provide adequate time for fathering.

Probably the most influential time-saving strategy for any father is the choice of a career. Career choice can make or break your fatherhood, especially since pressures from career demands tend to be extremely high during the childhood years – when your children need you most.

How do you choose a career that's helpful and not harmful to family life? Let's take as an example a man who wants to be a physician. Our man knows that he has the aptitude, interest, and necessary academic skills to be a physician. He also knows that his vocation (his calling from God) is to the sacrament of marriage as a husband and father. This man can make or break his family life simply by his choice of medical specialty. He can choose a specialty with a demanding schedule away from home many evenings and weekends, or he can choose a specialty that will enable him to be with his family on a more regular basis. His important choice of specialty will enable, or erode, thousands of hours of family time.

What if our man has already chosen a specialty and is in a demanding practice that keeps him from his family on evenings and weekends? A family-oriented physician could take on a couple of partners, thus creating the opportunity for weekend rotations. Whatever your job or profession, you can seek or create a niche that allows for adequate family time. You might not be able to switch immediately, but knowing what you want will help you see an opportunity as it arises.

When you consider various business positions, you can investigate the corporate culture for family-friendliness. Are the work hours required for promotions reasonable for a family man to assume? Are frequent family moves required for career advancement?

Out-of-town sales

Out-of-town sales work removes a father from the home almost every weekday and sometimes on weekends as well. What should a father in such a position do? If this job, or any similar type of employment, is necessary for family financial survival, there isn't much that can be done until an alternative arises. Some of the little time you do have might be spent studying in order to develop skills to become eligible for a promotion to a non-traveling position. Men in jobs with limited opportunities for changing schedules can continue to improve their skills while seeking a better position with a new employer.

Your commute & your children

Commuting decisions are also a major time factor in your fathering. Choosing a job without a long commute can give you as much as an extra hour each day with your family. Unfortunately, many dads don't consider family priorities when deciding where to live and work. It is important that you are regularly with your family for the evening meal. Extended hours coupled with long commutes can mean getting home just in time to kiss your young children goodnight – a setup for weak bonds with your children. A strong fatherhood is built upon regular daily contact with your children. If you count on just fathering on weekends and vacations, your children will grow up to form peer-based bonds stronger than your family bonds. By the time your children are pre-teens, you'll regret the formation provided by the peer group.

Sometimes prudential sacrifices in potential jobs need to be made, based upon your family and life priorities. When our family converted to Catholicism, I was left permanently unemployable as a Protestant minister. Sales in the marine industry was one career in which I felt I could succeed, making much more than I did as a minister. However, having been in the marine industry before the ministry, I knew such a position would kill weekends with my family and preclude any weekend apostolic work. I decided to forego this field to see if I could obtain a more family-friendly work opportunity. My other options were less financially rewarding, but more aligned with my family and life priorities. These decisions are tough to make, but hindsight usually shows clearly whether or not you made the right decision.

Having been a pastor in southwest Florida, I've had the opportunity to have meaningful talks with people who were approaching the end of life. It never ceased to amaze me that a man could summarize his high-profile career in a few minutes – and then describe in detail the lives of his grown children and grandchildren. Toward the end of our lives we will not have to struggle to discover valuable life priorities. They will be clear and unmistakable. Fathers with children still at home must insure that necessary career pursuits don't eclipse family life. Wisely choosing a career and job, along with the proper balancing of family and career, will give you a huge chunk of priceless fathering time.

Your "not to do" list

Every father has a "to do" list. But another strategy for saving large chunks of fathering time is maintaining a "not to do" list. For me, this is the hardest time-saving strategy to follow. I love taking on an exciting new project or challenge. Although it's easy to get into a new venture, it can require huge amounts of time and energy to fulfill it. It's impossible to endlessly add things to your "to do" list without harming your family life. The amount of time available to us is finite. Before you add something to your "to do" list, it would be wise to subtract something equally time-consuming. We must make hard choices on how to invest our time. Most of us regularly ask God in prayer about what He wants us to do. Recently, I've made it a regular part of my prayers to also ask what specific things He doesn't want me to do. Surprisingly, a few valuable projects that I was tempted to take on were added to my "not to do" list as a result of guidance resulting from prayer. One of life's biggest time-savers is learning how to say "No thank you," while under pressure to say "Yes."

Preacher's kids

Catholic fathers who over-commit themselves to parish service or apostolic work should take heed from the tragic "Preacher's Kid" (PK) phenomenon. It is common knowledge in Protestant circles that the minister's children are often the worst behaved children in the congregation. The reason is simple. The minister neglects to spend adequate time with them.

PK's fathers are usually highly dedicated men with great personal piety and tireless service to their churches and communities. But in their zeal to serve God they neglect their call to serve their own children. In the time commitment tug-of-war between Christian service and their children, the PKs usually get the short end of the stick.

It is vital for your children's spiritual formation that they see you in some form of active Christian service. Just beware that going overboard with service outside the home can be fatal to your fatherhood.

Little ways to find lots of fatherhood time

Wise fatherly time management involves not just exclusion of certain opportunities, but also inclusion of your children in existing activities, including sports. I like to jog after work, both as a way to stay in shape and to blow off some steam from the workday.

When children are young, they (hopefully!) go to bed early, so you only have a few hours between your getting home from work and their going to bed. Rather than coming home and immediately leaving my children while I went for a run, I bought a tandem jogging cart and took them with me as a simple way to include them in my workouts. I also took our dog, and invited my older children who could ride a bike to come along as well. Over a decade and a half, I have logged more than 10,000 miles on two- and three-mile runs with my children.

Why go to the gym after work if you have little ones waiting to see you at home? For less than an annual gym membership, you can purchase weights and a nice workout machine for a corner of your garage. I guarantee your little ones will want to spend some time with you during your workouts.

Take your children with you on Saturday trips to the hardware store and on your other errands. I've had some of the best conversations with my younger children while in the van doing Saturday errands. Yes, it's worth all the hassle of putting multiple kids in car seats. The quality time with Dad on Saturday errands is also worth all those trips to the bathroom in the backs of stores.

My travel to conferences seriously interferes with weekend activities with my children. I've discovered that wonderful lifelong memories are created when I take one of my children along with me on a weekend speaking engagement. If you receive one of my speaking packets, you'll notice that I ask weekend conference hosts to provide travel for a family member to accompany me. This arrangement doesn't solve all tensions created by weekend travel, but it certainly helps.

Whatever your situation, there are dozens of little ways of finding time for your children that, when added together, make a big difference in their lives. All it takes is a little creativity to incorporate your children into your daily life, your sports life, and your work life.

Closing the gap between thinking and action

There is a danger facing you right now. It is so easy to deceive ourselves into thinking that reading about a subject automatically translates into doing what needs to be done. Many, if not most, fathers fail to spend adequate time with their children – even though they say they wish otherwise. All of us need to close the gap between our desires for fatherly priorities and the actual accomplishment of them.

It might help to do annual, monthly, and weekly planning, especially in a prayerful context. During your planning, imagine you've just gotten news from your doctor that confirms that you have forty-eight months to live. What three things would you want to accomplish during your remaining months? Whatever these things are, they should definitely appear as priorities in your planner.

You may live long enough to be a grandfather, or even a great-grandfather, or you may die before the end of this year. Whatever your lifespan, if you practice living by priorities you'll die without regrets, leaving behind a legacy of faith and family.

You can't determine how long your life will be; that decision is out of your hands. Yet it is your choice how to use each day. The primary ingredient in successful fatherhood is "showing up." Yes, there are other important ingredients, but you don't need to seek a complicated fatherhood formula. You do need to show up.

CHAPTER THREE

Covenant Keeping:
The Foundation of Fatherhood

The single most vital component of fatherhood is a lifelong marriage. Why? We've already shown that successful fatherhood requires "showing up" – that is, sharing life by spending time with your children. Divorce typically causes a drastic reduction in a father's time with his children. After ten years of divorce, nearly two-thirds of children spend virtually no time with their fathers.[7]

For men, marriage and child-rearing are a package; they rise and fall together. If a man's marriage is severed, his fatherhood usually deteriorates. Many people, not wanting to face the fact that fatherhood withers after marital breakdown, advocate a program of strengthening fatherhood within a divorce culture. Such well-intended efforts are futile.

There is no escaping the fact that marriage is essential to successful fatherhood.

Consider just a few of the many devastating effects of divorce and fatherlessnes on children:[8]

- Twice the likelihood of emotional and psychological problems

- Lower academic achievement

- Higher incidence of being expelled from school or dropping out of high school

- Higher probability of drug and alcohol abuse

- Much more likely to live in poverty
- Higher levels of boys engaging in criminal activity and incarceration
- Daughters in single-parent homes are 164 percent more likely to have a baby out of wedlock[9]

Keep these statistics in mind the next time a friend (or even you) might be tempted to run off with a twenty-something secretary, or when the conflicts that occur within every marriage seem too much to endure. Divorce may seem to offer a quick fix for marital stresses, but a father's absence afterward causes a continuing negative effect on his children and has a cascading impact on the future generations of his family.

Unforeseen consequences

I heard about a Catholic man who boasted to his fishing buddies how he planned to dump his wife and marry a younger girlfriend, having been unwisely assured of an annulment beforehand. There are at least four things this man didn't account for. First, he was willfully breaking divine law, which entails eternal punishment unless sincerely repented of. Second, he was breaking the natural law; in doing so he forgot the lifelong consequences he was inflicting on his children. Third, within a few years, if not sooner, he would probably find out that his new girlfriend is more of a pain to live with than he ever imagined possible. (A girlfriend who is willing to take a man from his wife and children generally makes for a pitiful spouse.) Fourth, the power of his bad example will lead others to sin. In fact, the man who told me this story followed the example of his friend, leaving his own wife and children heartbroken.

If this was the negative effect on a fishing buddy, guess what the greater effect will be when this man's children experience a few rough spots in their marriages in the years ahead. Children of divorce have a high probability of following in their father's footsteps.

Parental divorce increases the likelihood of a daughter's marriage ending in divorce by 114 percent.[10] The seemingly quick solution of divorce carries with it a high probability of affecting a father's children and grandchildren.

Pope Leo XIII said, "Divorce once being tolerated, there will be no restraint powerful enough to keep it within the bounds marked out … Great indeed is the force of example, and even greater still the might of passion … The eagerness for divorce, daily spreading by devious ways, will seize upon the minds of many like a virulent contagious disease, or like a flood of water bursting through every barrier."[11]

All marriages experience ups and downs

Be aware that it is normal for all marriages to experience ups and downs, especially ….

- During the first decade of marriage
- For several months after the birth of a child
- When you have pre-school children in the home
- When a teen behaves in an extreme manner
- When a family member has a serious illness, or dies
- When you are unemployed or experiencing financial hardships

The good news is that the vast majority of marriages that just stick it out and grow through these tough seasons later become happy marriages. Seventy-seven percent of those couples who rated their marriage as "very unhappy" said that the same marriage was "very happy" or "quite happy" five years later.[12] Besides sticking it out through the rough spots, you can put your marriage on the path to happiness by taking steps to strengthen it.[13]

Steps to strengthen your marriage

Every marriage needs maintenance. Unfortunately, many guys take better care of their cars than they do their marriages. You could just run your car until it starts making noises, but if you wait until problems erupt you'll experience unscheduled interruptions in your transportation, coupled with some expensive repair bills. Most of us know the value of practicing preventive maintenance with our cars. Likewise, by practicing just a bit of preventive maintenance with our marriages, we can spare ourselves, our wives, and our children mountains of heartache.

In most communities there are annual conferences, workshops and seminars designed to strengthen marriages. When you hear of one, attend it with your wife.

Take time for your marriage

Most parents today are aware of the need to spend more time with their children. Are they equally aware of the need to spend time with each other, without the kids? Many two-career couples, homeschooling couples, and parents of pre-schoolers are often too exhausted for meaningful communication or even marital relations. Young parents often go for weeks (and sometimes months) without a date night. During these trying years, they need time together away from the children, even if it is just for a couple of hours. Get a sitter, get Grandma, or get an older couple to babysit, and get out together.

Avoiding the four marriage busters

There are four things that can increase the likelihood of divorce five- to ten-fold. Avoid these things at all costs if you value your marriage and fatherhood:

Marriage buster #1

Those who use artificial birth control have a probability of divorce ten times higher than couples who align their marital sexuality with the Creator's patterns.[14] What is it about birth control that causes such catastrophic divorce rates? To begin with, birth control is unnatural anytime it is used to thwart the procreative purpose of the sex act. Anytime we deviate from the Creator's design and intention, we run the risk of malfunction, whether it is our physical health, the health of our nation, or the health of our marriages. The divorce rate has skyrocketed 500 percent since the introduction of birth control in the early twentieth century and has doubled since the introduction of the pill in the 1960s.

Second, birth control is immoral. Every Christian denomination until 1931 strongly condemned birth control as immoral, a threat to the sanctity of marriage, and damaging to the souls of those who practiced it. When we engage in a serious sin, like birth control, we damage our relationship with God. Since the divine covenant and the marriage covenant are interconnected, any damage to our relationship with God is sure to show up in our relationship with our spouse.

Third, birth control is inescapably selfish. The marital embrace is designed by God to be a total giving of spouses to each other. When animals engage in reproduction, only their bodies are involved. God designed the marital embrace to be more than something just physical: it should be a total giving of persons to each other within matrimony. Each time spouses enjoy their marital embrace, they renew their love by this profound self-giving. With birth control, you selfishly take the pleasure, but don't engage in the total self-giving. This inevitably creates selfishness at the deepest level of your marriage. Selfishness is the opposite of self-giving love.[15]

If you have good reasons to limit or space births, there are ways to do this in harmony with God's design, without harming your marriage or violating moral principles. There is a natural method to limit or space births called Natural Family Planning.[16]

Marriage buster #2

Regularly viewing pornography is as dangerous as tossing a C-4 plastic explosive charge into the midst of your marriage. Pornography inevitably erodes the sexual bond between a husband and wife (it is usually noticed by the wife long before her husband thinks she notices). It also destroys trust and fidelity between spouses; frequently, it involves deceit and lying about activities and expenses. Since viewing pornography is a grave sin, it extinguishes grace in the soul, a spiritual condition sure to have effects on a Christian marriage.

I've corresponded with men losing their marriages to a porn habit that they picked up from their dads when they were boys. Don't leave a porn inheritance to your children and their families. If you have a problem with pornography, then take active steps to eliminate it from your life.[17]

Marriage buster #3

Alcoholism fractures thousands of families every year. Men who drink too much say and do things to their wives and children that they would never say or do while sober. Unfortunately, wives and children never forget the foolish things a man might say while drunk. Alcohol is fine if you can always use it in moderation; if not, then abstain – permanently. Your family is worth more than a bottle. If you have problems with alcohol, get informed and get help.[18]

Marriage buster #4

A father who lets himself become emotionally attached to a girl-friend will soon be saying goodbye to his wife and children. Any man can see that this is an incredibly stupid thing to do – unless he is blinded by temporary passion from a fleeting romance with a woman not his wife.

If problems cause a temporary separation between you and your wife, stay far away from girlfriends. Your marriage has an excellent chance of healing if you keep yourself away from emotional involvements, socializing with female co-workers, and visiting singles bars.

Take precautions at work. Don't share your personal problems and other intimate matters with female co-workers. It's how relationships start.

Take precautions during business travel. Don't travel alone with a female co-worker. Don't dine and socialize together on a business trip unless you are with a group of colleagues. If you are traveling alone, stay out of hotel bars.

Take precautions at the gym. If you can go to the gym daily and not sin with your eyes, you're a far better man than I. My recommendation: put exercise equipment in your garage.

Consequences of covenant breaking

God solemnly warns that breaking covenant with our wives will result in Him not even listening to our prayers. Carefully consider the sober warning given through the prophet Malachi:

> You cover the LORD's altar with tears, with weeping and groaning because he no longer regards the offering or accepts it with favor at your hand.
>
> You ask, "Why does he not?" Because the LORD was witness to the covenant between you and the wife of your youth, to

whom you have been faithless, though she is your companion and your wife by covenant ... And what does he desire? Godly offspring. So take heed to yourselves, and let none be faithless to the wife of his youth.

"For I hate divorce, says the LORD the God of Israel ... So take heed to yourselves and do not be faithless" (Malachi 2:13-16).

Covenant keeping: the greatest gift for your kids

The greatest gift you can give to your children is covenant keeping; that is, lifelong fidelity to the vows of your marriage. By taking prudent steps to strengthen and to guard your marriage, you're preserving the foundation of your fatherhood. If you keep His commandments, God promises to bestow covenant blessings on your descendants to a thousand generations.

Know therefore that the LORD ... keeps covenant and steadfast love with those who love him and keep his commandments, to a thousand generations (Deuteronomy 7:9).

This is a staggering promise for a legacy of faith in the generations of your family. Obey God, stay faithful to your promises, and God will stay faithful to His.

CHAPTER FOUR

The Power of Imitation:
A Father's Secret Weapon

I have a bad habit that I picked up years ago at military school. I was taught to spit shine, not the polite way with polish and water, but the old fashioned way with black Kiwi and spit. I thought nothing of my old habit until one evening during a meeting of the Wood Shoeshine Club.

Like it or not, I have an automatic shoeshine club whenever I shine my shoes. All I have to do is sit down with dirty shoes and polish and my younger children run to collect their shoes and join me. One memorable evening while I was (unconsciously) spit shining my shoes, I had to leave the room for a few minutes. When I came back into the room I discovered one of my daughters imitating my behavior – with a slight modification. If spit shining was good enough for Dad, then she felt "lick shining" would be even better. I stared in amazement at my three-year-old daughter licking her shoes. It was a rude awakening to the power of imitation that a father has with his children.

Fathers are often blind to the universal inclination of children to imitate them. Our children are *always* watching our actions, even when we are not aware of it. When my youngest son was two years old, my wife Karen found pennies in his dirty diapers. My son had observed that I put money in my wallet and then stuck it in my back pocket. Since he had no wallet or pocket, he just stuck loose change he found around the house down the back of his diaper. His wanting to be just like Dad with money gave new meaning to the expression "filthy lucre."

Once I consciously tried a "power of imitation" experiment. One of my daughters had a splinter in her foot and I needed to soak it in some Epsom salts. She was scared and very resistant to the idea of putting her foot in the bucket of warm water and salts. Her siblings nervously watched this first-aid mini-crisis unfold.

I had two alternatives. I could forcibly hold her foot in the bucket while she wailed for fifteen minutes, or I could try the power of imitation. I thought that if the secret of imitation worked in this tense situation it could work in almost any situation. Without saying a word, I took off a shoe and sock, rolled up a pant leg, and stuck my foot in the bucket. Immediately I found the formerly nervous siblings putting their feet in the bucket while roaring with laughter. My daughter with the splinter put her two feet in the bucket! Other than the problem of a crowded bucket, the power of imitation worked beyond all expectations.

Every child is a born imitator. Your children do not have to be trained to imitate observed behavior. They will do it automatically.

Fathers: icons of the Heavenly Father

Fathers have the simple yet challenging task of modeling in their own lives what they want to see reproduced in the lives of their children. They also have the solemn responsibility of being a type of living icon of the Heavenly Father for their children. John Paul II spoke of this, saying that the heart of fatherhood consists "in revealing and in reliving on earth the very fatherhood of God."[19]

Imitation is the way Jesus successfully trained His disciples, without ever taking them inside a classroom. Imitation is still the fundamental way to train Christian disciples. *The Imitation of Christ* by Thomas á Kempis is one of the greatest Christian classics. The title of this masterpiece describes the timeless essence of Christian living and discipleship.

As Christians we are to be imitators of God. We are to be merciful because God is merciful (Luke 6:36). We are to be holy because God is holy (Leviticus 11:45). We are to be kind and forgiving, because this is what God is like (Ephesians 4:32).

The important question for fathers is then, "How do I teach my children to imitate a God they cannot see?" Fathers are to be an image of the Heavenly Father for their children. Fathers are to live in such a way that their children can imitate their lives and grow in the likeness of God. Therefore, the most important thing needing change in the process of training children is not the kids, but the dads. Children *will* imitate the godly transformation of their fathers.

As a spiritual father, St. Paul said, "I became your father in Christ Jesus through the gospel. I urge you, then, be imitators of me" (1 Corinthians 4:15-16). He also said, "Be imitators of me, as I am of Christ" (1 Corinthians 11:1). Shouldn't we as fathers say the same?

Time and imitation

A wise father will seek to maximize the power of imitation in his children. This is a major reason why time priorities are so important. You need to be with your children in order for them to imitate you. Work and educational patterns in the modern world don't make this an easy task. The more you are separated from your children, the greater the vacuum left by your absence. Your children will continue imitating in your absence. The only question is, who will they be imitating? The time you spend with your children will determine whether they imitate your morals and beliefs, or someone else's.

The survival of a teen's faith in our post-Christian culture requires a consistent and courageous fatherly model to imitate throughout childhood. Remember, God has made children to learn beliefs and behavior from what they see.

Making your dent in the world

Most men want to leave their dent in the world. While there is nothing wrong with such a desire, it is important to carefully target where we want to leave our impression. Accumulating money and possessions, or achieving prestige and various positions, are vapors that diminish in importance even before we die.

In contrast, taking the time and making the effort to leave a godly image in the lives of your children will have an impact long after you're gone. Remember, your children will carry your influence to your grandchildren, and those children will grow up and pass it on to your great-grandchildren. Wisdom from the book of Sirach describes how the power of imitation passes on the father's legacy long after he is gone:

> The father may die, and yet he is not dead, for he has left behind him one like himself (Sirach 30:4).

The saints and imitation

The saints inspire imitation of their courage, obedience, faith, perseverance, sanctity, and prayerfulness. Read some biographies of the saints to your children. Keep pictures, statues, and icons of the saints in your home. Celebrate the feast days of the saints. All children need heroes and role models outside the family. In a world with so many bad role models, the lives of the saints are models for your children to imitate.

The virtues and imitation

Whenever you read a news report of someone who has done an exceptionally virtuous act, be sure to verbally affirm this person to your children. Let them know that you admire coaches and athletes who exhibit virtuous behavior. Recount the stories of those who selflessly put themselves in harm's way to defend others. Describe the service of priests and laymen engaging in mercy ministries to the poor. Good examples are always around us. Make it a point to notice virtuous behavior and bring it to the attention of your children.

Tim Gray, before he became a theology professor, developed an easy and highly effective method of teaching the virtues to reluctant high school students. Tim showed videos, like the old black and white *Titanic* movie, to his students. After the movies they discussed the outstanding virtues and vices portrayed by the various characters. These discussions left a deep and lasting impression on his students. You can do the same with your children.

The media & imitation

Since God has placed the inclination to imitate in children and teens, it is inevitable that they will behave like that which they see and hear through the media. Media experiences will dynamically affect their choice of clothing, vocabulary, attitudes, behaviors, and morals (or the lack thereof). The seeds from the media will sprout in their life. It is the ironclad law of sowing and reaping.

Flushing Nemo

A great movie for all ages was *Finding Nemo*, the tale of a clownfish captured and taken to a dentist's office aquarium. Nemo managed an escape by being flushed down a toilet into Sydney Harbor.

Following the hit movie, water treatment plants and plumbing companies across the country received frantic calls from parents wanting to know how to rescue the fish their children tried to liberate via flushing. One Roto-Rooter dispatcher in California received seventy such calls, many with kids crying in the background, wanting to know how to save flushed fish. The *Nemo* movie is a prime example of children imitating what they see in the media.

This is such an important topic that I'm devoting the next chapter to exploring ways fathers can manage the powerful influence of the media on their children.

5

CHAPTER FIVE

Media & Morals

The dynamic power of modern media exploits the power of imitation to such a degree that it can become a primary factor in the formation of a child unless there is careful monitoring by parents. Therefore, the power of imitation in the media demands that you defend your family from its relentless assaults. As St. Joseph took active steps to protect the infant Jesus from Herod, so you need to protect your children from Hollywood.

Best predictor of teen beliefs and behavior

Media input during childhood is one of the best predictors of teen beliefs and behavior. What children see when they are young is what they eventually start doing, especially as teens. Fathers should be aware that childhood media patterns are seldom improved during the teen years. If parents anticipate the teen years by establishing media monitoring policies during childhood, they have a baseline to work from during the inevitable testing of such policies when the child grows older. On the other hand, if the media are poorly monitored and managed during childhood, it is an excruciatingly difficult task to correct during the teen years.

During the teen years there is intense peer pressure to see the latest movie. A teen literally feels left out of a group experience if he doesn't see a popular movie, even if it is rated "R." Waiting to establish your media policy until late childhood or the teens is like trying to shift into reverse while traveling at seventy miles per hour.

Wise fathers need to respect the power of imitation for good or for evil. Dads need to develop their media strategies while their children are young, in order to keep the negative patterns of imitation from getting the upper hand.

No father likes it when his child shows disrespect, talks back, adopts sour attitudes, or disobeys. If movies and television don't continually reinforce these negative traits, parents have a good chance to correct such behaviors. Since you don't want your children to have Bart Simpson's smart lip and bad attitudes, or Britney Spears' sleazy wardrobe, why let them watch movies, cartoons, or television shows exhibiting such behavior?

The media's erosion of morals

We are in the midst of a massive explosion of sexual sin and decay of morals. The mass media over the course of the past five decades has effectively desensitized our consciences. It has led millions to accept mortal sin as something acceptable. Already it has normalized taking God's name in vain (a sin for which a person will not be held guiltless), divorce, fornication, sodomy, adultery, and cohabitation.

Many scenes in TV shows and in movies are intended to cause sexual arousal, or make immorality seem more and more acceptable. For your children to have any hope of living a pure life, they will need to be trained to make wise media choices. It was Jesus himself who warned that sexual temptations come through the eye (Matthew 5:28-29).

Three media strategies

Fathers facing this media onslaught usually respond with one of three general media strategies:

(1) Do nothing about the media and allow almost anything;

(2) Ban everything; or

(3) Monitor carefully and allow selective input.

The "allow almost anything" approach

Millions of Catholic parents take the first, "do nothing/allow almost anything" approach to monitoring the media. To simplify categorization, it is safe to say that any parent who allows his child or teen to watch MTV is in this category. Perversions and sadistic songs are regularly featured on MTV, the number one cable channel among twelve- to twenty-four year-olds. An MTV award night once drew a billion viewers worldwide. MTV broadcasts drunkenness and public nudity on spring breaks, and regularly features vulgarities and utterly deviant behaviors that are improper even to mention. And, here is the wakeup call for Catholic dads: Did you know that a higher percentage of Catholic youth watch MTV, and for longer periods of time, than even their non-Christian counterparts?[20]

Fathers who take the "do nothing" approach may not only see their kids lost in hell for eternity, they will most likely be joining them for their failure to protect. The "do nothing" approach so common among Catholic parents is unacceptable.

The "ban everything" approach

What about the second, "ban everything," approach? I have a friend who, in utter frustration with the trash on network TV, grabbed a steel pole and smashed the screen of his TV. His kids quickly got the idea that there wasn't going to be much TV in the house.

I must confess that I have often thought of doing the same thing. It appears to be a definitive and simple solution. Network television is toxic. Even if you find one of the few decent shows to watch, raunchy advertisements are randomly scheduled and difficult to monitor.

I fully respect those young parents who never introduce TV into their homes, as well as those families who get rid of it. This is definitely one of the two acceptable options.

Yet I would issue a caution to those taking the "ban everything" approach. Unless there is care exercised in implementing this, you are liable to encounter an extreme reaction as your children grow into later adolescence and their early twenties.

I first experienced "the reaction syndrome" in the 1970s, as a new Christian attending an Assemblies of God college. I couldn't figure out why my fellow students were consumed by attending second-rate movies when a dramatic youth awakening was taking place at a church three miles away. I discovered that, during the 1960s, the Assemblies of God taught that movie theaters were evil. One of my theology professors told me that after he sneaked in to see a Saturday afternoon movie, he called his mother to make sure that he hadn't missed the Rapture. He was taught that if the Rapture occurred while he was in the theater, he would be left behind.

I witnessed firsthand how church kids (and even pastor's kids) who grew up with the legalism of the sixties developed an obsession for what was strictly forbidden once they were away from home.

Don't think that such things happen only to Assemblies of God kids. Catholic parents who forbid all forms of contemporary music in their homes except classical and Gregorian chant would be utterly shocked to learn that many of their children, while away at an orthodox Catholic college, listen to utterly debased musicians.

Take, for instance, the musician Eminem, who advocates sex with family members, knifing prostitutes, drugs and hard liquor, suicide, murder, violence towards pregnant women, and killing with anthrax. He brags about his evil influence on youth. Did you know that Eminen is a favorite among millions of Catholic youth, including a substantial portion of those attending conservative Catholic colleges?

Dangers from being overly rigid and vocal

Parents who are overly rigid and vocal against the media may end up with young adult children without an internal media monitor, as the above examples show. Surprising research on alcoholism may explain the reason why.

Research has found that a parent going overboard against something tends to focus the attention of children on that thing, and eventually creates an obsession for it. The children of those who vehemently denounce alcohol have some of the highest rates of alcoholism. Therefore, if you don't want your kids to drink at all, the best approach is to be a *calm* abstainer.

The same principle applies to the media. If you choose to abstain from all TV and most movies, then it is probably wise not to make a big deal of it. Otherwise, you could be inviting an adverse reaction down the road.

The "selective input" approach

The third approach allows monitored and managed input of media. Allowing anything or nothing are simpler plans, but this third approach is worth consideration, even though it requires more effort to practice. The "allow almost anything approach" is unacceptable in today's world. The "allow almost nothing" and the "selective input approach" are the only two morally acceptable choices for your family's media policy. While your children are still young, it is critical that you and your wife make an informed decision regarding the media policy for your family.

What follows is a suggested outline of how the third "selective input" approach might be used to monitor TV, movies, computers, music, and advertising in your family.

Unplugging network television

Network and cable television, with just a few exceptions, is poisonous to children. It is probably easiest and wisest to eliminate network television. If there is a particular show that has merit, then pre-record it so you can speed through ads. If you watch football and other sports on TV, then you need to have the remote control in hand to switch off the ads. Don't even bother tuning in for the halftime show.

Instead of constant access to network TV, have movie nights on weekends. This eliminates TV for the better part of the week without forbidding it altogether. It also frees time for schoolwork, hobbies, and evening reading.

It is a poor idea to have a TV in a child's or teen's bedroom, especially if it is connected to cable or an antenna. There is no way to monitor what is watched.

Evaluating movies

Before allowing your children to watch any movie you are unfamiliar with, go to one of the many excellent Christian web-sites that reviews movies for objectionable content. I generally like to read two evaluations by reliable sources before giving an okay to a film.[21]

As your children get older, you'll want to avoid a "my tastes" vs. "your tastes" tug-of-war in choosing movies. Third-party movie reviews with specific criticisms offer an objective basis for you to forbid an objectionable film.

After my teens observed my consistent use of movie reviews, they started going to the websites themselves. If the reviews are favorable, they print them out for me to read when I get home. If the reviews are unfavorable, then the matter is often dropped without my having to say "no." Following this pattern also gives children a learning experience in how to evaluate various forms of the media.

Filtering films

A few scenes having profanity, nudity, sensuality, or excessive violence ruin countless movies that would otherwise be acceptable. After recent technological advances, there is no longer any reason to endure bad language, nakedness, sex scenes, or excessive violence when your family watches a movie. Digital audio and visual filtering for DVDs enables viewing movies without the crud. Rapid technological changes are constantly offering better filtering options.[22]

Guarding against pornography

Internet pornography has grown to be the biggest moral challenge to Catholic men, teens, and boys. It has lured millions of Catholics into its addictive snare. Viewing online porn causes a bio-chemical reaction, imprinting the image in the brain for decades to come. Increasingly degrading types of porn are required to maintain the same level of chemical stimulation, thus assuring a progressive slide into unimaginable degradation.

Pornography has invaded every parish in North America. It has infected Catholic colleges and schools, homeschooling families, and youth groups. Twelve- to seventeen-year-old boys are among the highest consumers of pornography. Pornography is downloaded in schools and libraries, and copies are passed along to friends via CDs. The average age for first exposure to pornography is eight.

How can you protect your children against this onslaught? As with TVs, place computers connected to the Internet in an open location in the home. Install both filtering software (preventing visits to bad sites) and accountability software (making a record of questionable

Internet visits).[23] Be proactive about Internet pornography and obtain some resources to help your sons maintain their sexual purity.[24]

Our website for fathers has an extensive collection of resources for men and boys to maintain sexual purity, to gain freedom from pornography, as well as tools to increase Internet safety.[25] Since computer and communications technologies change so rapidly, you need to keep alert to the latest in safe media resources.

Visits to friends' and relatives' homes

Visits to friends' and neighbors' homes can quickly undermine your careful media monitoring. Your child could end up playing video games with profanity and sexual innuendos, watching unacceptable movies, or even viewing porn on a friend's computer. For instance, many older children have access to the popular video game *Grand Theft Auto*. A part of the "game" includes picking up a prostitute and having sex with her in the back seat. After the sexual encounter, the "game" allows you to save a few bucks by beating the prostitute to death with a baseball bat to avoid paying her.

Be safe, and avoid exposing your children to such trash by encouraging them to play outside as much as possible at neighbors' homes, weather permitting. If they do get together indoors, you need to know beforehand all media choices, and if a responsible parent is monitoring what is being viewed. Better yet, have them play at your house where you know what they're playing.

In addition, I recommend that you pre-approve any movies seen on overnight visits to friends' and relatives' homes. If, during an overnight, someone suggests a movie that was not pre-arranged, ask your child to call home for approval before watching. Unfortunately, even with Christian parents, you cannot assume that other homes share your media standards.

Monitoring the mailbox

Amoral advertisers think nothing of mailing full-color displays of women in lingerie, or placing full-color semi-nude inserts in the local newspapers. Any man or boy desiring to maintain sexual purity needs to avoid these ads. The entertainment sections full of Hollywood sleaze should not be left around the house for children to read.

School-aged children have a God-given sexual latency period. This means that unless disturbed, their interest in sex is dormant. Once a child's latency is violated, it is impossible to restore. Parents should be wary of all forms of advertising which are sexually suggestive, or explicit.

The musical minefield

Children and teens spend more time each day listening to music than they do watching TV. Millions of Christian children and young adults spend hours each day listening to music that explicitly advocates and extols mortal sin.

You should not permit your child or teen to listen to secular heavy metal music. Here is an excerpt from a Free Congress report on the names of 238 heavy metal rock groups:

> There are at least 13 bands named after the male genitals, 6 after female genitals, 4 after sperm, 8 after abortion and one after a vaginal infection. ... [There are also] at least 10 bands named after various sex acts, 8 including the F-word.[26]

Heavy metal isn't the only type of music that must be avoided. The typical Top 40 radio playlist isn't harmless entertainment. In the lyrics of songs on Top 40 radio are references to all types of explicit sex including fornication, porn, date rape drugs, oral sex, and sodomy. Songs frequently mention the abuse of women, violence, drugs, alcohol, and suicide.

What about the so-called "harmless" pop music, like that of Britney Spears? Britney's performances feature suggestive moans, gyrations and undulations to her audiences of pre-teen girls and their mothers. Here are a few lyrics from Britney's aptly titled song "Toxic":

> I can't wait, I need a hit, Baby, give me it. With a taste of your lips, I'm on a ride, You're toxic I'm slipping under, With a taste of a poison paradise, I'm addicted to you...It's getting late, To give you up, I took a sip, From my devil's cup, Slowly, It's taking over me.[27]

What amazes me is that parents are distressed when their pre-teen Britney-fan daughters insist on wearing tight and skimpy clothing, especially midriff-baring shirts and skirts. What did these moms and dads expect when they allowed their daughters to be exposed to such media? Predictably, their daughters are just trying to imitate their media idol.

Contemporary Christian music

Parents strictly forbidding all contemporary music in the home will have a high probability of success during childhood and maybe even during the early teen years. Nevertheless, the important question is, "What do the majority of children raised this way listen to while driving, away at college, or during young adulthood?" My estimate is that less than ten percent will follow their parents' pattern. If parents are overly strict during childhood, the musical choices at college often gravitate to the worst forms of rock.

I realize that many may disagree with me, but parents may want to consider exposing their children to some contemporary Christian music during older childhood and the early teen years. If Christian young people don't adopt a contemporary musical alternative, I'd estimate that there is a high probability that they will be listening to large doses of the worst forms of secular rock music. I realize that many parents may not like the beat of some contemporary Christian music, or may have strong preferences for classical music. Yet these same parents would be heartbroken if their teen or twenty-something adopted a regular diet of debased rock.

I make the above suggestion in light of the times we are living in. I encourage parents to consider what I have written; however, you and your wife need to make your own realistic, prudent, and wise decision. Whatever musical strategy you adopt, decide on it long before problems with musical choices arise.

In the thinking of most Catholic teens and young adults who take their faith seriously, there is a dangerous divorce between the choice of music and spiritual life. In defense of their questionable choice of music they might say, "I like the beat and I don't listen to the lyrics," or "The lyrics don't affect me." Is it true that lyrics just bounce off us, or do they eventually find a permanent home in our minds? The lyrics do matter, just as what we see on television and in movies matters.

The next media frontier

The media is preparing us for the new frontier – the moral degeneracy that accompanies the normalization of sodomy. Already there is a 24-hour–a-day youth homosexual cable channel. An aggressive and pervasive media onslaught is flooding our children with images, songs, words, and so-called role models normalizing homosexuality and stigmatizing anyone against it. The media will also lead the effort to criminalize as "hate speech" any criticism of homosexual behavior. Schools will urge children to report to authorities their parents and pastors who might dare to utter a word against sodomy.

In large part due to the media's perverse and pervasive influence, many students in Catholic high schools and colleges already believe that there is nothing wrong with oral sex or sodomy.

Raising pure kids in an age of apostasy

Do you hope to keep the greatest apostasy in human history from recruiting your children? If so, then you are going to have to monitor the media. Parents have the duty to ensure that the use of the media in the family is carefully regulated. Left unmonitored, it is the mortal enemy of your children's souls. Manly courage, determination, foresight, wisdom, and prudence are all needed to form an effective battle strategy that will save your children from this deadly peril.

CHAPTER SIX

The Education of
Your Children

It is critical for the long-term welfare of your children to carefully analyze our cultural situation before making the educational choice between parochial, public, private, or homeschool. The Old Testament speaks of the men of Issachar "who had understanding of the times, to know what Israel ought to do" (1 Chronicles 12:32). Cultural analysis needs to precede educational decisions if you want to avoid nasty surprises during the later teen years.

If you believe that we are living in basically normal times with just the usual struggles between good and evil in our culture, then your educational choices will likely include traditional classroom education.

If a good Catholic school is available in your area, then that should be your first traditional classroom choice, as long as you can afford it. But when choosing a school, don't just opt for any Catholic school. Some Catholic schools are riddled with negative peer pressure, modernism, feminism, values clarification, classroom sex education, and gay and lesbian training. Your kids are better off in an average public school (one that's likely to be free of potential shootings and physical assaults) than a bad Catholic school. You don't want them growing up thinking that the Catholic faith was truly represented by their deficient Catholic school experience.

If you believe that we are experiencing a cultural decay of historic proportions, then you will want to seriously consider homeschooling. The reason stems from the inescapable fact that toxic cultural currents are brought into even the best schools. Again, I'm not criticizing the many good schools and the thousands of excellent teachers. The debased culture is the problem, and it is nearly impossible to keep it out of schools.

I know of one solidly orthodox Catholic grade school whose teachers are some of the finest in the United States. Yet during bathroom breaks some of the children were imitating the immoral sexual behavior of a former occupant of the White House.[28] This wasn't the school's fault. Rather, it was the almost inevitable result of students bringing to the school the immoral values and practices they absorbed from the wider culture.

Peers inevitably bring undesirable aspects of the culture to the school playground, lunchroom, bus, and other places where teachers cannot closely monitor behavior and conversations. I know of another conservative elementary school where pornography was passed among the boys on the playground.

Many parents are deceptively lulled into a false sense of security by their child's seeming ability to survive in an anti-Christian peer culture. Despite this, after a decade of immersion the peer culture usually gains its hold. By the time parents realize what's happened, their seventeen-year-old has embraced hedonism, rejected their authority, and spurned the Faith. In desperation, such parents search for the magic bullet to reverse what has been done. When parents in this situation contact me, I urge them, if they have younger children, to take immediate action to ensure the same thing doesn't repeat itself.

I'll offer my analysis of our times, realizing that some (even many) will reject my conclusions. Yet believing as I do, I'd be a moral coward not to share my thoughts. You are free to disagree with my analysis of the times. That's fully your choice – and your solemn responsibility. All I ask is that you carefully consider our cultural status before deciding on the educational choice for your children.

Return to paganism & the new Dark Age

From a Christian point of view, I don't believe that our culture is in the process of collapsing. Rather, it has already collapsed – we are in a post-Christian era that has returned to paganism. I further believe that the pagan era we have entered will end up darker than pre-Christian paganism. Having turned our backs on the light of Christ, our culture has willfully made a choice for darkness. The divine punishment for such a choice is that God allows us to experience its bitter fruits.

What are some signs of the times? Forty million surgical abortions over the past three decades, along with ten times that many chemical abortions from birth control chemicals and devices; homosexuality out of the closet and on the front pages and the big screen; debased sensuality and pornography everywhere; sodomy in seminaries; Catholic bishops covering up a pedophilia/predatory homosexual crisis; Protestants ordaining homosexuals; state and national initiatives for same-sex marriage; the infectious spread of classroom sex education; and groups like the National Association of Catholic Diocesan Lesbian and Gay Ministries (NACDLGM), are just a few of the indicators of where we are as a culture.

James Dobson remarked that it seemed to him like someone has gotten hold of the world's rheostat and turned the lights down. For those who agree with him, we need to ask, "What's the source of all this moral darkness?" It is my *personal* belief, informed by the vision of Pope Leo XIII, that Satan has been unchained and freed from the abyss with his demonic host in an historic attempt to deceive the world.[29] In a nutshell, I believe that we are living in times like the days of Noah, when "the wickedness of man was great in the earth, and that every imagination of the thoughts of his heart was only evil continually" (Genesis 6:5).

Building an ark for the salvation of your family

The Bible says, "Noah ... took heed and constructed an ark for the saving of his household" (Hebrews 11:7). If you are in agreement with my analysis that our culture has collapsed into a new Dark Age, then you need to consider providing education within your family. The ark saved Noah's family, even though they lived in a culture that was about to be destroyed. Homeschooling, while certainly not a cure-all for every peer and cultural problem, may indeed be the ark for the saving of your household.

Homeschooling should be considered by every family as a means of guarding children from the negative cultural influences emanating from the peer social environment in traditional schools.[30] A benefit of homeschooling is that it allows children to have a genuine childhood without being overwhelmed with the problems of a degenerate culture, until they have the maturity to face it. These children can serve as leaders in transforming secular culture once they are properly educated and have matured.

We don't send children into physical combat, nor should we send them into grave moral combat. It is foolish to expect a child to be able to combat degenerate cultural influences before they have received the Sacrament of Confirmation, before they are steeled by really knowing the Faith, and have reached some maturity of years. Homeschooling should at least be considered for a child's most formative grade school years.

I realize that many families, for a wide variety of reasons, are not able to homeschool. I don't want any family incapable of homeschooling to feel "pressured" to homeschool. I do believe that it is the best option, but the homeschooling option is not available in everyone's circumstances. Husbands should never try to force reluctant wives into homeschooling. It's far too difficult a task to accomplish for any length of time without a strong internal motivation to do it. On the other hand, a husband should be extremely cautious about dampening his wife's desire to homeschool.

Those willing and able to embrace homeschooling will find that it transforms their family. Dr. Mary Kay Clark, founder of the worldwide Seton Home Study School, has said, "Homeschooling is more about home than schooling." She's right. More than homeschooling's educational achievements (although they are notable), the primary benefit is the deepening of family ties.

The family motel

Too many modern homes are often like a "family motel" where members park their cars for the evening, grab a bite to eat (often individually), and consume entertainment and sleep before heading off on their separate ways the next day. At "family motels," work, education, spiritual development, and recreation take place somewhere other than at home.

Homeschooling has an amazing capacity to reverse a two century decline in the home's centrality, because it restores a vital social function to the family: namely, the education of children. The return of education to the home inspires a stronger and deeper life lived within the family circle. Such a domestic transformation will dramatically increase your parental influence in the lives of your children. It's obvious that your wife will have much more time for maternal influence. But as a father, you'll find that homeschooling deepens *your* commitment to your children as well.

Socialization: peers or parents?

During my youth ministry experience, I repeatedly saw the damage done to Christian teens by the peer group. Many fear a socialization deficit if they homeschool their children. I believe that the opposite is the case. The massive problems with adolescents in western nations stem in large part from socialization by the peer group instead of parents. If you doubt my words, then I'd urge you to peek in on a (public or parochial) high school dance, or visit your local mall after 10:00 P.M. Ask yourself, "Is this the type of socialization I want for my child during his or her teen years?"

From my training in keeping teens off drugs, I learned that the secret to overcoming peer pressure was replacing it with parental pressure. I just didn't know of a practical way to provide adequate amounts of parental influence during childhood, that is, until Karen and I discovered homeschooling as new parents. Homeschooling seemed to be an ideal way to prepare for the inevitable challenges posed by the threat of the teen peer group. Our family has been homeschooling for the past eighteen years, from kindergarten right through high school. Homeschooling certainly hasn't eliminated parenting challenges, but it does help minimize them. For both Mom and Dad, homeschooling is one of the best ways to replace peer pressure with parental influence.

A University of Florida study showed that kids schooled at home don't lag in social development and are better behaved. Why? In the words of the study, "homeschooled children behave better because they tend to imitate their parents, while traditionally schooled children model themselves after other children in the classroom."[31] In other words, the power of imitation is at work both in homeschools and in traditional schools. The only question is, who is the pattern for imitation: parents or peers?

Will they become misfits?

Many men wonder if their children will turn out to be misfits if they are homeschooled. For men wrestling with this question, I suggest a visit to the "Home School Hall of Fame" that honors men who were partially, or totally, homeschooled.[32] Some of those men include:

- Presidents: George Washington, Thomas Jefferson, James Madison, John Quincy Adams, Abraham Lincoln, Theodore Roosevelt

- College Presidents: John Witherspoon (Princeton), Timothy Dwight (Yale), William Johnson (Columbia)

- U.S. Supreme Court Chief Justices: John Rutledge, John Jay, John Marshall

- Scientists/inventors: Blaise Pascal, Thomas Edison, Benjamin Franklin

- Authors: Mark Twain, C.S. Lewis

- Generals: Stonewall Jackson, Robert E. Lee, Douglas MacArthur, George Patton

Can homeschoolers play ball?

Homeschoolers' ability to play sports is a primary question for many fathers. Although homeschoolers have crossed most of the academic hurdles with ease, they are only starting to make their presence felt in sports.

In at least fourteen states, homeschoolers can "walk on" a high school field or court to play varsity sports. The NCAA has given full status to homeschooled students and has given them eligibility to receive sports scholarships at Division I colleges.[33]

Some homeschooled athletes include:

- Katie Hoff, a 2004 Olympic swimmer and the youngest member of the U.S. team in Athens. In 2005, she won the gold medal in the 200 meter world swimming championships.

- Kevin Johnson, University of Tulsa basketball, All-Western Athletic Conference, 87 double-figure-scoring games, team leader in rebounds and blocked shots

- James "Bubba" Steward, teenage motocross champion, one of the first African-American champions in any major motor sport. Stewart holds the record for most career amateur national championships. He is reported to earn $4 to $5 million on the professional circuit, while still a high schooler. *Sports Illustrated* predicts he is "destined to change the face of Supercross." When asked if he missed going to high school he replied, "No way!" He initially wanted to go to high school, but is now happy getting an education and racing on the professional circuit[34]

- Kyle Strait, mountain bike champion, was beating pro racers while he still needed his mother to drive him to races

- Robin Graham, the youngest person to sail around the world

- Jason Taylor, homeschooled through high school, played football for the University of Akron, and is a veteran defensive end with the Miami Dolphins. A terror to opposing quarterbacks, Taylor led the league with 18½ sacks in 2002. Jason Taylor has earned numerous honors, including: All-Pro honors, three time Pro Bowl performer, All-NFL Defensive Teams.

Homeschooling and family finances

Except for divine grace, every good thing has a cost that must be carefully weighed in light of deeply-held priorities. Homeschooling several children can be an expensive financial decision, since there will not be a full-time second paycheck for two decades.

On the other hand, it could be a costly mistake to place your children in a peer setting that erodes their faith and morals.

The decision to survive on a single paycheck in today's unfriendly-to-the-family economy will require sharpening one's breadwinning skills, radical avoidance of unnecessary debt, and wise financial management.[35]

Before making the costly decision to homeschool, it is wise to concentrate on deepening one's family priorities first. It is only with a clear understanding of our times, coupled with divinely infused grace, that you will make wise decisions about the education of your children.

If you believe, as I do, that our culture has reached toxic levels fatal to children, then you need to take the necessary steps to minimize toxic peer culture. You shouldn't do this just as an attempt to escape from worldly influences, but primarily to enable your children to develop normally, until they reach maturity and can engage the world as leaders of the Church Militant.

CHAPTER SEVEN

Training Your Children to Obey Your Voice

Training your children to obey your voice is an essential task of fathering. When many people consider child training and discipline they think about spanking. Yet the central focus of discipline is the ear, not the rear.

Citing the Fourth Commandment, St. Paul highlights the essential duty of children to honor their parents by obeying them:

Children, obey your parents in the LORD, for this is right. "Honor your father and mother" (this is the first commandment with a promise), "that it may be well with you and that you may live long on the earth" (Ephesians 6:1-3).

The Catechism says, "Respecting this commandment provides, along with spiritual fruits, temporal fruits of peace and prosperity. Conversely, failure to observe it brings great harm to communities and to individuals."[36] Therefore, training your child to hear, respond, and obey your voice is significantly related to his temporal and eternal well-being.

The Greek word for obey (*hypakouō*) in Ephesians 6:1 is a compound word that literally means "to hear and to respond." In other words, the essence of obedience is not just the sense perception of hearing, but also attention to, acceptance of, and response to what is spoken. For a word picture of what it means to obey, think of a person hearing a knock at the door, and responding by going to the door and opening it.

Such obedient hearing was foundational to the spirituality of Israel as expressed in the great *Shema* (from the Hebrew word "to hear") in Deuteronomy 6:4-5:

> "**Hear**, O Israel: The LORD our God is one LORD; and you shall love the LORD your God with all your heart, and with all your soul, and with all your might."[37]

The pious Jew would recite the *Shema* at least twice daily. It was (and is) repeated in the home and in the synagogue.

Israel's refusal to listen

The sad story of Israel's decline, fall, and deportation into captivity stemmed from their failure to listen and obey the voice of Yahweh. In His rich mercy, God sent the prophets in an attempt to win a hearing and response. When ancient Israel refused to listen obediently to God, He permitted terrible consequences to overcome the nation. Zechariah says that, when the Israelites cried out in the midst of their trials, God refused to listen to their pleas because they had previously refused to listen to Him.

> But they refused to hearken, and turned a stubborn shoulder, and stopped their ears that they might not **hear**. They made their hearts like adamant lest they should **hear** the law and the words which the LORD of hosts had sent by his Spirit through the former prophets. Therefore great wrath came from the LORD of hosts. "As I called, and they would not **hear**, so they called, and I would not **hear**," says the LORD of hosts, "and I scattered them with a whirlwind among all the nations which they had not known. Thus the land they left was desolate, so that no one went to and fro, and the pleasant land was made desolate" (Zechariah 7:11-14).

In the Old Testament there is a parallelism between the destiny of the nation and the individual. Both are promised blessings if they hear and obey.

Blessing to the nation that listens

"And if you **obey** [listen with obedience – same Hebrew word as "hear" in Deut. 6:4] the voice of the LORD your God, being careful to do all his commandments which I command you this day, the LORD your God will set you high above all the nations of the earth. And all these blessings shall come upon you and overtake you, if you **obey** the voice of the LORD your God. Blessed shall you be in the city, and blessed shall you be in the field" (Deuteronomy 28:1-3).

Blessing to the son who listens

Hear, my son, your father's instruction, and reject not your mother's teaching; for they are a fair garland for your head, and pendants for your neck (Proverbs 1:8-9).

Hear, my son, and accept my words, that the years of your life may be many (Proverbs 4:10).

And now, my sons, **listen** to me: happy are those who keep my ways. **Hear** instruction and be wise, and do not neglect it. Happy is the man who **listens** to me, watching daily at my gates, waiting beside my doors (Proverbs 8:32-34).

Consequences of Israel's refusal to listen

"But if you will not **obey** the voice of the LORD your God or be careful to do all his commandments and his statutes which I command you this day, then all these curses shall come upon you and overtake you" (Deuteronomy 28:15).

This same dreadful pattern occurs in the life of individuals as well as nations.

Consequences from a young man's refusal to listen

Wisdom cries aloud in the street; in the markets she raises her voice ... "Give heed to my reproof; behold, I will pour out my thoughts to you; I will make my words known to you. Because I have called and you refused to listen, have stretched out my hand and no one has heeded, and you have ignored all my counsel and would have none of my reproof, I also will laugh at your calamity; I will mock when panic strikes you, when panic strikes you like a storm, and your calamity comes like a whirlwind, when distress and anguish come upon you. Then they will call upon me, but I will not answer; they will seek me diligently but will not find me. Because they hated knowledge and did not choose the fear of the LORD, would have none of my counsel, and despised all my reproof, therefore they shall eat the fruit of their way and be sated with their own devices. For the simple are killed by their turning away, and the complacence of fools destroys them; but he who **listens** to me will dwell secure and will be at ease, without dread of evil" (Proverbs 1:20-33).

The critical forty-eight months

A wise father takes full advantage of the forty-eight month window when his child is between two and six years old to ac-complish basic training for a lifetime of responsive listening. The contest for your child's ear is won or lost during these months: the foundation of your child's basic willingness to listen and respond, or to refuse obedience, is cast during this window of opportunity. Certainly, the rest of childhood and the teen years require further development and consistent follow-up, but the basic attitude toward listening forms quickly – just like concrete. Make sure that you spend adequate time with your children during these months, and take full advantage of the "tender years" to train your child's ear.

When I was a son with my father, tender, the only one in the sight of my mother, he taught me, and said to me, "Let your heart hold fast my words; keep my commandments, and live; do not forget, and do not turn away from the words of my mouth" (Proverbs 4:3-5).

How to determine when to begin training for listening

When your son or daughter is up and navigating around the house on two legs (between 18 and 24 months old), he or she is almost ready for basic training in listening. Give your child a simple test to make sure that he can understand basic requests. For example, ask your child to go to another room and retrieve a specific object, like a rainbow-colored ball. It might help to place a few different colored balls in the same room before making this request. If your child comes running back to you with a big smile and the rainbow-colored ball, then you know that he can easily understand simple words like "No" and "Come."

Beware of selective hearing failure

One morning my wife, while looking directly at my youngest son, said, "Come." He just stood there motionless, looking at Karen with an "I-don't-understand-English" expression. Karen wasn't sure what to do, since Matthew might not have understood her words. Later that same day, she overheard a backyard obedience training session between eighteen-month-old Matthew and our dog, Misty. Matthew repeatedly and sternly said, "Misty, come!" and motioned for the dog to follow him. His cover was blown. From that day on, Matthew was required to come when called.

Remember, children are smart and they will use any technique they can think of to throw you off balance once you start issuing commands to them. My favorite as a boy was to stare at my mother and pretend that I didn't even hear her. Unfortunately, it cost me more than one visit to the pediatrician to have my hearing checked.

Don't play baseball when training the ear

Every baseball hitter deserves three strikes before he is called out, but don't play baseball like so many parents mistakenly do when training the ear to obey. Parents fully determine whether their children obey the first time, second time, or more. If you say, "This is the third time I've warned you," then your children will come to expect zero consequences until you make three requests. If you want your children to respond to your voice the first time, then insist on obedience to your words at the first request. Avoid second or third warnings and nagging.

Commit and re-commit to consistency

Make a commitment that you will not give a command unless you are prepared to follow up on it. Let your words be few, but insist on one hundred percent obedience to whatever you say.

Most parents have a tendency to become lax in requiring responsive listening to a first request. It is helpful for Mom and Dad to have parental pow-wows once or twice a year to recommit to their children's character training, especially in requiring responsive and obedient listening. A couple of weeks before school starts in the fall is a good time for parents to recommit themselves to teaching first-time responsiveness.

Don't be a volcano

Parents inevitably get very frustrated after a few hours of playing "three strikes and you're out" every time they want their children to do something. Many just give up trying to get their kids to obey unless it is something important, and then they blow up in anger. At that point the kids scramble to do whatever their parents had requested. Unfortunately, some kids take this as a lesson that parents aren't really serious about obedience until the volcano erupts.

The sixty second secret to getting your kids to obey

How would you like your children to respond to your voice the first time – well, at least most of the time? The secret to training them to value your words is to value them yourself.

Picture yourself just having slipped into your La-Z-Boy recliner, ready to start reading about your favorite team in the sports pages. It has been a hard day at work and you're tired. You've waited all day for these few peaceful moments. Out of the corner of your eye you notice that your four-year-old son, Bobby, is about to hit your two-year-old daughter on the head with a toy they have been fighting over. As you glance over your paper you say, "Bobby, don't you dare hit your sister over the head."

Now Bobby is a perceptive four-year-old. He notices that Dad is in the full recline position, lost in the sports pages. He says to himself, "No real threat here," as he proceeds to bop his sister over the head. Dad, what you do in the next sixty seconds will determine in a significant way what Bobby will be like years from now.

After Bobby hits his sister, a wise dad would keep his eyes on him while he slowly and deliberately folds his sports section and pulls the La-Z-Boy into the upright position. He moves to Bobby and kneels down looking straight into his eyes and says, "Bobby, you didn't listen to my voice." After telling him the importance of listening, Bobby receives a proper amount of discipline. The important lesson here is that even though Bobby thought nothing of his dad's warning, his dad thought enough of his own words to sacrifice a few moments of personal pleasure and relaxation in order to model for his son the value of the command.

A father can also help his son value his mother's voice. Picture the same scenario, except the mother notices Bobby's assault about to begin. She says, "Bobby, don't you dare hit your sister." Bobby, the ever-perceptive son, notices that the microwave is beeping, the newborn in his mother's arms is crying, and something is boiling over on the stove. What is his split-second analysis? He perceives no consequences as he proceeds to hit his sister. About this time Dad becomes aware of what just transpired, and he is out of his chair, looking straight into Bobby's eyes, saying with a stern and concerned voice, "Bobby, you just refused to listen to your mother's voice." Again, the important lesson for Bobby, besides any disciplinary measures he received, is the way his father's actions demonstrated the value of his mother's words.

Once you have convinced your children that you are willing to inconvenience yourself to back up your words, you'll find that you will have to inconvenience yourself less and less often. Most of the time after giving a direct instruction, your children will glance your way to see if you are taking your own words seriously. All you have to do is fix your gaze their way for a few seconds while sending the non-verbal signal, "Yes, I'm attentive to what I just said and I am ready and willing to back it up if needed." Ninety percent of the time, three or four seconds of your special gaze will gain compliance.

If you have several children, with the older ones already knowing that Dad will follow through with spurned requests, it can get even easier. During the few seconds the child is deciding whether or not to obey, your older children will see you with that "look" and say to the younger child, "You better do it!"

Preventing teacher burnout

The number one reason for homeschool burnout is a lack of discipline in the home. Homeschooling is tough work for any mother, and having the additional emotional weight from disobedience becomes too much for many homeschooling mothers.

When I was in school there usually was a coach, acting as an assistant principal who handled serious discipline problems for teachers. At my school, the coach and his paddle (i.e., board of instruction) were very effective. Ouch! After the one time I was sent to him, I made sure that I never returned.

Thirty years ago, I headed a large Christian education ministry in Southern California. I was responsible for recruiting and staffing teachers. It was a difficult job keeping teachers, because they were always quitting due to discipline problems. To solve this problem, I told the teachers that I would take responsibility for the more troublesome discipline problems. The number of teachers quitting dried up to a trickle. Equipped with a new discipline book by a young UCLA professor (James Dobson), I found that I could cope with the problems.

How to correct problems from the office

When Karen and I started our homeschool, I decided to follow a strategy similar to the one that I used in my Christian education ministry. I told her to call me at the office if she encountered any serious discipline problems and that I would drive home and settle the problem. Some of my children tested the policy to see if I would actually follow through. I did. They quickly learned that it wasn't in their best interests to upset Dad and make him take time off from work and drive home to discipline them. After demonstrating my commitment to deal with discipline problems by coming home, I found that a phone call from the office could correct most problems. I simply ask the children if we can handle the problem over the phone, or does the situation require my presence at home. They usually choose the phone option. In fact, a reluctant student often finds the necessary motivation for proper behavior as Karen reaches for the phone to call me.

Training for the teen years

In Proverbs 1:8, the father exhorts his son to heed the voice of his parents, and in the next several verses warns him not to heed the voice of sinful peers. The wise father knows his son will experience the pull of the peer group. Therefore, he arms his son in advance by alerting him to the enticing voices of peers, and exhorts him to listen to parental instruction instead. A father who trains his son's ear in early childhood and nurtures this training throughout childhood is equipping his son with one of the most effective countermeasures to the allures of the teen peer group later in life.

Protection from loose women

If the inducement of the peer group vs. parental instruction is a tug-of-war for an adolescent, then the enticement of the loose woman is a tractor pull. When the father in Proverbs warns his son about the seductive speech of the loose woman, he prefaces his warnings with an encouragement to heed his voice.

> My son, be attentive to my wisdom, incline your ear to my understanding; that you may keep discretion, and your lips may guard knowledge. For the lips of a loose woman drip honey, and her speech is smoother than oil; but in the end she is bitter as wormwood, sharp as a two-edged sword. Her feet go down to death; her steps follow the path to Sheol (Proverbs 5:1-5).

> My son, keep my words and treasure up my commandments with you; keep my commandments and live, keep my teachings as the apple of your eye; bind them on your fingers, write them on the tablet of your heart … to preserve you from the loose woman, from the adventuress with her smooth words (Proverbs 7:1-3, 5).

Training for eternity and for withstanding the apostasy

In utterly significant ways, the simple training of your child's ear in your family room, kitchen, or backyard, is training not only to withstand mortal sin, but training for walking on the path that leads to heaven. Jesus warned that those who just listened to His words, but didn't couple their listening with obedient action, didn't really know Him. He taught that only those who heard and obediently responded to His words would obtain eternal life (Matthew 7:13-27).

As St. Paul in 2 Thessalonians describes the events leading up to the day of the LORD, he predicts that before the second coming there will be a massive apostasy (that is, a falling away from the Faith) throughout the Gentile world. Cardinal Ratzinger (now Pope Benedict XVI) said, "We are living through an apostasy from the faith. It is as if the connection between European-American culture and Christian culture were being dissolved."[38] During an apostasy, mortal sin seems acceptable since "everyone is doing it." Thus, the Gentiles toward the end of time will have their hearing tested, just like Israel in the Old Testament. St. Paul solemnly warned:

> When the LORD Jesus is revealed from heaven with his mighty angels in flaming fire, inflicting vengeance upon those who do not know God and upon those who do not obey [Gk. *hypakouō*, lit. listen and respond, same word as in Ephesians 6:1 for children to obey their parents] the gospel of our LORD Jesus. They shall suffer the punishment of eternal destruction and exclusion from the presence of the LORD and from the glory of his might (2 Thessalonians 1:7-9).

Training your young child's ear to obey is critical for a time of apostasy, for their entire lifetime, and even unto eternity. May every Christian father have the wisdom to teach his children how to have ears to hear the voice of parents and the Word of God.

> Give ear, O my people, to my teaching; incline your ears to the words of my mouth! (Psalm 78:1).

CHAPTER EIGHT

To Spank,
or Not to Spank?

Perennial debates about the propriety of spanking abound. Anti-spanking advocates publish reams of psychological studies attempting to document extensive harm from spanking, while the media attempts to portray spanking as the companion of heinous forms of child abuse.

Despite decades of anti-spanking propaganda, the majority of parents continue to spank, at least occasionally. In 1997, eighty-one percent of adults said they were spanked as children, almost the exact number when the same question was asked fifty years earlier.[39]

Complicating matters is the sharp divide within the Christian community. Pious believers line up on both sides of the debate with sincerely held reasons for their position. How is a parent to sort through all this?

A simple question:
the key to solving the spanking debate

To solve any difficult problem, it helps to have a question that probes to the heart of the issue. Answer the following question and you'll make progress toward resolving the spanking dispute: "What are the fundamental and pervading sources of authority to use as guides in resolving this dispute?"

Almost every committed Catholic leader dealing with the spanking question would claim to have Sacred Scripture, Sacred

Tradition, papal teaching and Church councils as the sources of their authority. Yet this assertion only goes halfway. As Catholics, these sources of authority are not only to be a part of our thinking and decision making, but they are to pervade the process.

There is a serious flaw in the thinking of many Catholics with degrees in both psychology and theology. Unknown to many of these persons is the fact that their studies in psychology have distorted some areas of their theology. While sincerely believing they are presenting Catholic viewpoints, they are actually reading things into their religious beliefs that originated in secular psychology. Most people with this flaw are completely unaware that their thinking has been colored by a humanistic psychology.

Therefore, parents need to be discerning whenever they consult the advice of a Christian psychologist. While there are many good ones, many others should be avoided.[40] There are great blessings flowing from a genuine Christian psychology, but troubling consequences stemming from a psychologized Christianity.

If you allow Sacred Scripture, Sacred Tradition, papal teaching, and Church councils to pervade your thinking and decision making, the spanking question is very easy to answer.

What does the Old Testament say about corporal punishment?

The Old Testament is unmistakably clear in showing that just as God the Father chastises the wayward children of Israel, so earthly fathers are to discipline their children.

Know then in your heart that, as a man disciplines his son, the LORD your God disciplines you. So you shall keep the commandments of the LORD your God, by walking in his ways and by fearing him (Deuteronomy 8:5-6).

My son, do not despise the LORD's discipline or be weary of his reproof, for the LORD reproves him whom he loves, as a father the son in whom he delights (Proverbs 3:11-12).

He who spares the rod hates his son, but he who loves him is diligent to discipline him (Proverbs 13:24).

Discipline your son while there is hope; do not set your heart on his destruction (Proverbs 19:18).

Folly (foolishness) is bound up in the heart of a child, but the rod of discipline drives it far from him (Proverbs 22:15).

The rod and reproof give wisdom, but a child left to himself brings shame to his mother (Proverbs 29:15).

Do you have children? Discipline them, and make them obedient from their youth (Sirach 7:23).

He who loves his son chastises him often, that he may be his joy when he grows up. He who disciplines his son will benefit from him (Sirach 30:1-2, NAB).

Is the Old Testament teaching obsolete?

There is overwhelming evidence for corporal punishment in the Old Testament. So how do anti-spanking "experts" dodge this clear teaching? One child "expert" holding a prestigious archdiocesan position claimed that the Old Testament is unfit as a pattern for discipline. She even said that the Old Testament is unsuitable for reading to children. Not only this "expert," but many contemporary Catholics, claim that the God of the Old Testament is a warmongering ogre, unlike the loving God of the New Testament. Although they are probably unaware of it, proponents of such a negative view of the Old Testament are repeating the ancient heresy of Marcion, who rejected the Old Testament.

The Catechism says that Christians should venerate the Old Testament (all 46 books) as the true Word of God. "The Church has always vigorously opposed the idea of rejecting the Old Testament under the pretext that the New has rendered it void (Marcionism)."[41] Furthermore, the Catechism says, "The books of the Old Testament are an indispensable part of Sacred Scripture" and these "writings are a storehouse of sublime teaching on God and sound wisdom on human life." [42]

Anyone who automatically trashes all these Old Testament verses is way off base. Christians have no right to say, "That's Old Testament stuff," and proceed to forget about it.

The Catechism does say that the books of the Old Testament "contain matters imperfect and provisional."[43] Yet it is up to the teaching Magisterium of the Church – not psychologists, sociologists, or educational specialists – to tell us what these provisional things are.

If Old Testament teaching is upheld by the New Testament and in the teaching of popes, Church councils, and catechisms, it is beyond question that these discipline verses stand for our day.

Pope Pius XI and discipline in Proverbs

Pope Pius XI taught with magisterial authority in his encyclical, *On Christian Education,* when he wrote, "'Folly is bound up in the heart of a child and the rod of correction shall drive it away' (Proverbs 22:15). Disorderly inclinations then must be corrected, good tendencies encouraged and regulated from tender childhood..."[44] What could be more authoritative than a papal encyclical citing the continuing relevance of Proverbs' teaching on corporal punishment? The opinion of a psychologist does not outweigh a papal encyclical.[45]

St. Thomas Aquinas and corporal punishment in Proverbs

St. Thomas Aquinas, a doctor of the Church, taught in his *Summa Theologica* the continuing validity of discipline as taught in Proverbs:[46]

> It is written (Proverbs 13:24): He that spareth the rod hateth his son, and further on (Proverbs 23:13): Withhold not correction from a child … Hence when parents are forbidden to provoke their children to anger, they are not prohibited from striking their children for the purpose of correction, but from inflicting blows on them without moderation.[47]

Pope Pius XII on the discipline of children

Until the outbreak of World War II, Pope Pius XII gave weekly addresses to newly married couples in Rome. Here is what he said to the newlyweds about discipline:

> Take care … not to wait until your children are grown up before exerting your authority over them carefully and calmly, but at the same time firmly and frankly, not giving in to any display of tears or temper. From the very earliest days, from the cradle, from the first glimmer of reason, see to it that they experience the touch of a loving and gentle but wise, prudent, vigilant and energetic hand. [48]

Is the New Testament silent on corporal punishment?

Ephesians 6 and Hebrews 12 are explicit about a father's duty to discipline [chastise] his children:

> Fathers, do not provoke your children to anger, but bring them up in the discipline and instruction of the LORD (Ephesians 6:4).

The *Friberg Greek Lexicon* says that the Greek text of Ephesians 6:4 refers to fatherly discipline, punishment, and correction as a reflection of God's fatherly discipline. [49] The lexicon then refers to Hebrews 12:5 as a parallel passage.

Fatherly discipline in Hebrews 12

Besides saying that the Old Testament verses on discipline are obsolete, the biggest biblical blunder made by anti-spanking advocates is to say that the New Testament never mentions corporal punishment. Apparently they haven't studied the New Testament carefully, since Hebrews 12 explicitly cites Proverbs 3:11-12 to demonstrate how (in both testaments) God the Father and earthly fathers discipline, chastise, and punish their children. In the quotation below, the bold text is the quote from Proverbs 3:

> And have you forgotten the exhortation which addresses you as sons? – **"My son, do not regard lightly the discipline of the LORD, nor lose courage when you are punished by him. (6) For the LORD disciplines him whom he loves, and chastises every son whom he receives."** (7) It is for discipline that you have to endure. God is treating you as sons; for what son is there whom his father does not discipline? (8) If you are left without discipline, in which all have participated, then you are illegitimate children and not sons. (9) Besides this, we have had earthly fathers to discipline us and we respected them. Shall we not much more be subject to the Father of spirits and live? (10) For they disciplined us for a short time at their pleasure, but he disciplines us for our good, that we may share his holiness. (11) For the moment all discipline seems painful rather than pleasant; later it yields the peaceful fruit of righteousness to those who have been trained by it (Hebrews 12:5-11).

It is difficult to comprehend how a person could miss the importance of discipline and chastisement in the New Testament after reading Hebrews 12.

Verse 5 in the Hebrews 12 passage quoted above begins with the question, "Have you forgotten the exhortation which addresses you as sons?" Apparently, many contemporary Christians have forgotten the exhortation. When verse 7 describes the Heavenly Father's discipline, it clearly assumes that every earthly father disciplines his son. In fact, for God or for a dad, not to discipline a son would be to treat him like a bastard. Conversely, discipline (even the painful type) is a mark of genuine fatherly love (vss. 6, 7 & 11).

Verse 9 mentions that filial respect is a valuable by-product of a father's discipline. We are living in a climate where only the love, mercy, and kindness of God are mentioned, while the justice, holiness, and fear of God are widely neglected. The result of such an imbalance is that God the Father Almighty gets little respect and obedience. Later in Hebrews 12, it mentions that the Old *and* New Covenant way to approach the Almighty God, who is a consuming fire, is with reverence and awe. We are exhorted to heed His voice, a voice that literally has the power to shake the universe.

We live in a day when most Christians believe that the way to heaven is broad and the road to hell is narrow. Jesus taught the opposite (Matthew 7:13-14). In a culture like ours, where very few people expect to go to hell, there is no fear of God: consequently, sin runs rampant. If there was a reverential fear of God, there would be millions fewer practicing homosexuals, cohabiting fornicators, pornography viewers, and adulterers. The right methods of child discipline and catechesis are not a cure-all, but they will help protect your child from succumbing to a life of sin.

Consequences of a failure to discipline

Children who experience a modest dose of painful, yet loving, discipline may have a greater chance of missing hell. Proverbs 23:13-14 urges parents not to withhold correction from a child, since the rod will help deliver their children from hell. Children need to learn before they are five years old that there are painful consequences to sinful actions. Otherwise, they'll have a good chance in their teens and twenties to swallow an increasingly popular lie: that habitual and unrepentant sinners go to heaven.

St. John Chrysostom, also a doctor of the Church, exhorted parents by saying, "Let them learn from their first youth that there is a Judgment, that there is a punishment; let it be fixed in their minds. This fear being rooted in them produces great good effects. For a soul that has learnt from its first youth to be subdued by this expectation, will not soon shake off this fear."[50]

St. John Chrysostom said that the thought of hell will cause young people to walk righteously and that neither the struggles of youth, nor the temptation of riches, nor an orphan state, nor any other thing, will be able to overcome it once it is fixed in the mind.[51]

Does Jesus punish anyone?

I once received a paper written by a "conservative" Catholic psychologist arguing that since Jesus didn't punish anyone, parents shouldn't use corporal punishment. Such flawed and pitiful exegesis (biblical interpretation) goes far to prove that a sincere child-rearing "expert" armed with a degree in social work and a bit of theology is as dangerous as a Civil War physician. Yes, it is true that Jesus didn't punish anyone at his first coming (except the whip of cords he used on the moneychangers), but he did repeatedly and solemnly warn that, at his second coming, he would be sending multitudes straight to hell for an eternity of unspeakable corporal punishment in unquenchable fire.

Enter by the narrow gate; for the gate is wide and the way is easy, that leads to destruction, and those who enter by it are many (Matthew 7:13).

And do not fear those who kill the body but cannot kill the soul; rather fear him who can destroy both soul and body in hell (Matthew 10:28).

And if your hand causes you to sin, cut it off; it is better for you to enter life maimed than with two hands to go to hell, to the unquenchable fire ... And if your eye causes you to sin, pluck it out; it is better for you to enter the kingdom of God with one eye than with two eyes to be thrown into hell, where their worm does not die, and the fire is not quenched (Mark 9:43, 47-48).

These verses sure sound to me like Jesus is warning that hell is going to have radical corporal (bodily) punishment, and lots of inhabitants. How could anyone who has glanced at the Gospels come up with the flawed theory that, since Jesus didn't punish anyone during his earthly ministry, he is therefore against corporal punishment – and thus we should be too?

Yes, I am aware of the pious nonsense (which sadly receives a wide hearing) questioning whether anyone will actually end up in hell. We live in a day when the majority of Catholics are living in grave sin and heading for hell, yet at the same time, ironically, hell's realities are deemphasized.

Liberal theologians are some of the most naïve people on the planet. They seem to fall for the craziest notions, even if they are contradicted by the explicit teaching of our LORD himself, as record-ed in the Gospels. Fathers can't afford to follow blind theologians denying hell's realities – otherwise the deep ditch they and their children could fall into will be hell for eternity.

The ultimate good stemming from the occasional temporary pain associated with discipline, lovingly applied, is much more than merely avoiding hell. The chief blessing is that it helps us to share in God's holiness and righteousness, thereby preparing us to live with our Heavenly Father as sons and daughters for eternity (Hebrews 12:10-11). Your choice of discipline methods for your children will have lasting consequences. Choose wisely, and in accord with the Scriptures and the historic teaching of the Church.

Temporal divine punishments

Rabbis in the Old Testament era developed the view that divine correction was a privilege of God's children. The unbelieving Gentile nations were left in temporal prosperity which would eventually lead to final ruin.[52] The New Testament continues this theme in Hebrews 12, Revelation 3, and 1 Corinthians 11, where chastisement is a mark of divine sonship.

During the present age, Jesus mercifully chastises those he loves. To the lukewarm church in Laodicea Jesus warned, "Those whom I love, I reprove and *chasten*; so be zealous and repent" (Rev. 3:19). Revelation 3, like Hebrews 12, makes a clear connection between God's love and his chastening.

St. Paul said to Christians in the church at Corinth who were partaking of the Eucharist without self-examination, "But if we judged ourselves truly, we should not be judged. But when we are judged by the LORD, we are *chastened* so that we may not be condemned along with the world" (1 Corinthians 11:31-32).

The *Theological Dictionary of the New Testament*, the standard worldwide reference for Greek word study, calls the chastisement in 1 Corinthians 11:32, "an outflowing of fatherly love."[53] Christian fathers are following the Heavenly Father when they moderately and lovingly chastise their disobedient children. Fathers are not to take a therapeutic approach to child discipline, but rather they are to model their discipline after that of God the Father. God chastises so that his children avoid eternal condemnation and grow in holiness. Should Christian fathers do any less?

St. John Chrysostom's warning to fathers who fail to discipline

St. John Chrysostom warned otherwise pious fathers of eternal punishment, if they did not follow Ephesians 6:4. He said:

"Let us bring them up in the chastening and admonition of the LORD." If a man who has unruly children is unworthy to be a Bishop (Tit. 1:6), much more is he unworthy of the kingdom of Heaven. If we have … unruly children, shall we have to render account? Yes, we shall … for our own individual virtue is not enough in order to [attain] salvation.[54]

This solemn warning is not a solitary fluke. In other homilies, this saint and doctor of the Church made it plain to fathers that "virtue in ourselves suffices not for our salvation, but we must take with us others [wives and children] too."[55]

Stern warning from *The Catechism of the Council of Trent*

In a similar fashion, *The Catechism of the Council of Trent,* the official catechism of the Catholic Church for over four centuries, also warned timid parents with the example of Eli. This catechism was issued by the express command of the Council of Trent, and carries at least the same authority as a dogmatic Encyclical.[56] *The Catechism of the Council of Trent* says:

Should a fault be committed which requires reproof and chastisement, the parent should not, on the other hand, by undue indulgence, overlook its correction. Children are often spoiled by too much lenity and indulgence on the part of their parents. The pastor, therefore, should deter from such excessive mildness by the warning example of Eli [Heli], the high-priest, who, on account of over-indulgence to his sons, was visited with the heaviest chastisements (1 Samuel 2). [57]

Read 1 Samuel 2 to see exactly what kinds of eye-opening chastisements Eli suffered for his defective fatherhood, before you blindly follow the latest in contemporary psychology.

Catechism of the Catholic Church

The new universal Catechism's commentary on the Fourth Commandment explains parental duties associated with education and correction in section 2223. The text of this section cites Sirach 30:1-2 and Ephesians 6:4:

> He who loves his son will not spare the rod … He who disciplines his son will profit by him.

> Fathers, do not provoke your children to anger, but bring them up in the discipline and instruction of the LORD.

The juxtaposition of these two verses in the context of the Catechism's commentary on the Fourth Commandment is clear and authoritative Catholic teaching: good parents may use corporal punishment. Even though most Catholic anti-spanking advocates will try to duck the unambiguous teaching of the Scriptures in section 2223, at least they should stop their condemnations of the use of spanking by loving parents. They should also cease their continual association of moderate spanking with child abuse, striking, and excessive severity. The Catechism doesn't do it, so neither should they.

What about those saints who didn't spank?

In the history of the Church, there have been saints who have managed orphanages and ministered to children that never practiced spanking. Are the examples of these saints to be used as a normative pattern for Catholic parents?

As a general rule, we are to follow the example of the lives of the saints. If I were running an orphanage today, I would probably follow the example of these saints and wouldn't spank the children under my care. In fact, there may be no choice in the matter since civil governments in most jurisdictions would not allow it. Yet we need to be careful that we are comparing apples-to-apples and not apples-to-oranges. A saint, or anyone working in an orphanage raising an orphaned child who is not his own biological descendant, is not in the same category as a parent raising a child.

Don't get confused in the spanking debate by similar but different situations. The Church (popes, Church councils, catechisms, and doctors of the Church) has spoken clearly, authoritatively, explicitly, and repeatedly to parents about corporal punishment.

Big brother will criminalize spanking

Parents need to be aware of totalitarian efforts on the part of the UN Committee on the Rights of the Child which is pushing for legislation in nations throughout the world to make spanking children a violation of human rights. Already the European Convention on Human Rights has ruled that spanking is a violation of a child's human rights. At least eight countries have outlawed corporal punishment.

As international organizations, trans-national courts, and human rights commissions grow in strength you should anticipate spanking to be criminalized. It will be okay to kill babies through abortion, let children view pornography, euthanize sick children, and teach about homosexuality in school, but loving parents who spank will be tried as child abusers. Eventually, children will be asked to report to school authorities any parental violations against "human rights" in their homes. The United States may hold off these international initiatives for a time, but it will not be immune to Big Brother's interventions into family life. The road ahead will not be an easy one for Catholic parents.

Summary

The timeless, consistent, and uninterrupted teaching of the Scriptures, catechisms, papal encyclicals and exhortations, and the angelic doctor, St. Thomas Aquinas, is that corporal punishment is a duty of fathers.

9

CHAPTER NINE

How to
Administer Discipline

Administering discipline, especially spanking, can be like a see-saw. It's easy not to do; yet if you do decide to practice it, it's easy to go too far. A moderate balance is required to avoid both mildness and severity.

While St. Paul exhorts fathers to discipline their children in Ephesians 6:4, he prefaces it by saying, "Do not provoke your children to anger." Any dad can provoke his children to anger by disciplining them excessively, or while he is flaming angry. Such acts are extremely counterproductive.

Just like St. Paul balanced his exhortation to discipline with a caution against excessiveness, the *Catechism of the Council of Trent* warns against going overboard with discipline:

> In the first place, they are not by words or actions to exercise too much harshness towards their children. ... Hence (the pastor) should require parents to avoid too much severity and to choose rather to correct their children than to revenge themselves upon them. [58]

You should *never* hit your children, or use spanking as an outlet for a violent temper.

If you're angry, wait to discipline

While Pope Pius XII recommended spanking in his advice to newlyweds, he also warned about disciplining in anger:

> If at any moment you do not feel that you are altogether in control of yourselves, postpone until later, at a better time, the rebuke or punishment which you feel to be necessary. Your punishment will have a far different effect, a more authoritative and instructive influence, if your spirit is firm but undisturbed, rather than excited by poorly-controlled emotions…[59]

Spanking when your anger is out of control is dangerous – it could lead to harming a child. Therefore, if you are heated, wait until you calm down before administering corporal punishment. Ephesians 6:4 warns fathers about "provoking your children to anger" in the context of discipline. If you spank in anger, you will build a wall of bitterness between you and your child. In contrast, discipline done with moderation and love will build bridges to your child.

How to keep from disciplining in anger

Every parent knows that it is easy to get angry when children misbehave. It is helpful to have a set procedure, with several steps that you must follow before spanking your child. By following a set of steps before the spanking, you are giving yourself the necessary time to calm down and get your anger under control. You also keep yourself from taking a quick, angry swat at your child that you will later regret.

Here are a few steps in the discipline process that you may want to follow. First, walk with the child to a special room, lock the door for privacy, and calmly repeat the offense to the child. If possible, try to get your child to acknowledge the wrongdoing before spanking. Explain that it is your responsibility to discipline for such willful acts of disobedience, and then spank. After the spanking, include a prayer asking for God's forgiveness for the disobedient act and then have a hug. If this is done properly, you and your child should feel closer than before the spanking.

For some men, the time necessary for these few steps will be adequate to keep anger under control. Other men will need longer periods of time for their adrenaline to calm down. The more prone you are to anger, the more steps you need to give yourself. No matter how long it takes, wait until you are fully under control before spanking your child.

What should I do if I discipline my child in anger?

If you discipline your child in anger, then you should do one of the hardest things in the world. You should privately apologize to your child. It is the supreme ego-killer for a parent to have to apologize to a five-year-old for an angry response. Yet your apology will keep the channels open with your child. You will be teaching them, by example, the virtue of humility. You will also be teaching them how to reconcile with someone they have offended. This is a tool your children can use later in life to maintain a healthy marriage.

Three types of men who should never spank

First, if for whatever reason you always seem to lack control over your emotions when you try to discipline, then you shouldn't spank. This is how child abuse occurs. Let me repeat myself: if you can't spank without anger and harshness, then don't spank. Included in this category are men raised in abusive homes, who find themselves repeating the sporadic blow-ups and abusive anger they experienced when growing up.

The second type of man who should never physically discipline is an alcoholic. Alcohol often causes men to express their emotions excessively and physically. This is a recipe for abusing a child (or spouse). If you've had too much to drink, then don't spank. I'm convinced that the negative reaction to corporal punishment in many circles stems from angry alcoholics hitting their children.

The third type of man who shouldn't spank is a stepfather of a child whose natural father is still alive. Stepfathering is loaded with complications and conflicts in child rearing. Spanking a stepchild, especially a child whose father is still alive, will usually provoke a strong, angry reaction.

The need for parental unity

It is essential that you and your wife agree on the methods and types of discipline that you will use. Pope Pius XII said:

> Be careful, too, not to allow the least sign of disunion to appear between you, or any difference in the way each of you treats your children. They quickly learn how to use their mother's authority against the father's, or the father's against the mother's, and they can hardly resist the temptation to take advantage of these differences in order to satisfy their own whims.[60]

Although most couples postpone developing their discipline strategy until their first child is about two, it is wise to make these decisions before having children.

What's the "rod" spoken of in Proverbs?

You probably noticed that the word "rod" is mentioned in several of Proverbs' discipline verses. A rod refers to any small neutral object used to spank, like a wooden spoon, or ruler. Never use an object that can physically harm a child, and never use it to spank a child anywhere other than the rear end. Some parents spank using an open hand on the rear end; others prefer to use a neutral object, so that a younger child doesn't confuse spanking with hitting.

Never, ever, strike your child with a fist. This is child abuse.

Taming the terrible twos

Spanking should start early in a child's life, so that the rebellious self-will is subjected to the parents' authority. Yet a spanking should not take place before a child is capable of understanding the words you are using and the rules you are enforcing.

You'll discover that at around two years of age, your child begins in earnest to exert his will. You'll frequently hear him say, "I do it myself." Most of such expressions should be encouraged. Your child should increasingly be given ample opportunities to make his own decisions. But a direct and defiant challenge to parental authority should be lovingly disciplined. If such challenges are firmly met, there should be no such thing as "the terrible twos."

Temper tantrums

Temper tantrums are outbursts of the frustrated self not having its demands met. The easiest way to cure temper tantrums is to nip the very first one in the bud. Don't be taken by surprise in seeing "your precious baby" burst out in his first tantrum. Rather, you should surprise him at his first tantrum with an unexpected level of loving and firm discipline.

Reasons to spank & not to spank

A child should *not* be spanked every time he acts up or disobeys. You should use spanking only in a few situations where the severity of the discipline required merits a spanking. Here are a few situations where a spanking might be used:

- a willful, outright, and defiant challenge to parental authority
- a flagrant disrespect for those in authority
- a stubborn refusal to obey
- a refusal to forgive, ask forgiveness, or reconcile

I do not believe a spanking is merited for:

- an offhand word or act where sincere remorse is expressed and forgiveness is sought
- mistakes, accidental spills, and breakages
- refusing to eat certain foods

The seriousness of unforgiveness

There are many childish offenses that are easily corrected without a spanking. A child's refusal to forgive is not one of them. In our home, a persistent refusal to forgive and reconcile is a spanking offense.

Although many Christians casually ignore His words, Jesus said, "If you do not forgive men their trespasses, neither will your Father forgive your trespasses" (Matthew 6:15). In the parable of the unmerciful servant, Jesus again warned that there is no forgiveness from heaven if there is no forgiveness in our hearts toward others. This means that unforgiveness can lead to a loss of heaven. A wise father will insist that forgiveness is extended in his household. This important life lesson should be learned before the child is five years old. Learning to forgive will also contribute to the success of your child's future marriage.

Discipline with consistency

Do not spank your child in an outburst of anger for refusing to obey your voice if you have allowed him to continually ignore your instructions. Consistency in training his ear to obey will keep the need for spanking to a minimum.

Sporadic blowups are counterproductive in producing godly children. Your children need the secure boundaries formed by calm and consistent discipline. Often you need to make the effort to discipline your children when you don't feel like doing it, like when you are tired, busy with some project, watching a game, or when you have guests.

> He who spares the rod hates his son, but he who loves him is diligent to discipline him (Proverbs 13:24).

What should I do with the child who always needs discipline?

Remember that children need just as much love and affection as they do discipline, if not more. Sometimes children are disobedient in order to fulfill their need for attention from their parents. Other times children are disobedient because they are lacking in esteem. More time spent giving your children positive and loving instruction will usually reduce the need for corrective discipline. Discernment is needed to be sensitive to your child's needs. Place this child near you at the dinner table. Give this child a special nickname that is descriptive of your affection. Children who need extra doses of spanking also need extra doses of your affection.

Steady at the helm with a strong-willed child

I've had concerned parents of a strong-willed child call me with grave doubts about their child's possibility of ever making it to heaven. I reply that I have great confidence that God's grace can and will work through the hearts of strong-willed children. I know because I was one. In fact, these children may grow up with the backbone necessary to stand up against the peer group, and they often end up being Christian leaders.

A parent of a strong-willed child needs an inner resolve and certainty like that of a captain of a ship during a ferocious storm. If the captain exudes a quiet confidence that the ship will get through the storm, then the crew will absorb his confidence. On the other hand, if the captain shows just a slight uncertainty, then his fears will be magnified in his crew. As a father, your captain-like confidence will be absorbed by your strong-willed child. Just be steady at the helm through the strong-willed storm.

Blindsided by the compliant child

Parents are often too concerned for a strong-willed child and not concerned enough for the compliant child. Once the strong-willed child finally gets the rebelliousness out of his system, he usually settles down to a successful Christian life.

Some compliant children, who are almost headache-free for their parents during childhood, erupt in rebellious behavior in their late teens or twenties. Parents experiencing this say, "What happened?" Well, it is the same thing that happened to their strong-willed child, except that this rebellion is coming out later in life. To minimize the chances of this late-blooming rebellion, don't overlook the occasional acts of disobedience by your compliant children.

The diminishing need for spanking

The need for spanking, if done properly, should have a diminishing frequency. A father who finds himself spanking all the time is doing something wrong. Your child is smart. If he knows that you will back up your words with a spanking, then spankings are rarely needed. His attitude adjusts without spanking, yelling, or mounting frustration. Often, simply locking your gaze into his eyes when he is acting up will serve as an adequate correction.

Older children, who have been raised knowing that Dad will spank if obedience isn't forthcoming, will often warn their younger siblings. When they see a spanking brewing, they'll tell their younger siblings that Dad will spank and that they'd better obey. A wise father will just keep his eyes fixed on the situation and allow a few seconds for the sibling warning to sink in. Most often this is all that is needed to correct behavior.

The reluctant wife

I know of a Catholic family, typical of many, where the father wanted to spank his sons for their ongoing rebellious behavior, but his wife strongly objected to the idea. Month after month the mother struggled, trying to manage her disobedient and disrespectful sons. Finally, in desperation, she agreed that the boys needed a spanking.

She was stunned by the sudden transformation in her sons after a single spanking. When her boys knew that their dad was ready with a spanking if they disobeyed, they didn't disobey, and the atmosphere of the home was much happier.

Just remember that decisions about child discipline should be joint marital decisions.

What about adopted children?

There is an urgent need to expand adoptions in all countries where abortion is running rampant. For Catholic parents to adopt children in most parts of the world today, they have to agree not to spank their adoptive children. Most adoption agencies view even moderate and restrained forms of spanking as child abuse. If I were adopting a child, I would probably go along with these regulations in order that a child could go to a Christian home.

After I spoke on spanking at one of my conferences, an older father approached me.

I quickly sized him up, guessing that he was a non-spanking advocate and was going to give me a piece of his mind. He surprised me. He said that he and his wife had adopted two children, in addition to having a few children of their own. He described how one of the adopted kids did something significantly wrong – and the child knew it. With hesitancy, he spanked the boy. Right afterwards, the child said, "Now I know that I'm *really* one of your kids."

This adopted boy gave an eloquent commentary on the discipline passage in Hebrews:

> It is for discipline that you have to endure. God is treating you as sons; for what son is there whom his father does not discipline? If you are left without discipline, in which all have participated, then you are illegitimate children and not sons (Hebrews 12:7-8).

Despite this unforgettable encounter, I would refrain from spanking an adopted child if it would jeopardize an adoption. If the law allowed, I would spank a child adopted at an early age, treating him just as I would a biological child.

Differences in discipline with boys and girls

After passing through a few decades of the myopic view that there are minimal differences between boys and girls, recent research is turning such thinking on its head.[61] The discovery was made that girls often responded well to verbal discipline that instructed them to imagine themselves from the perspective of the person being harmed. Such an approach fell flat with boys, who responded best to authoritarian discipline that included the necessary occasional spanking.[62] I can't speak firsthand for girls, but I can testify that my father's authoritarian discipline was needed during my boyhood.

What's wrong with a slap across the face?

A decade ago, a Georgia mother was arrested and charged with felony cruelty to children for smacking her nine-year-old son across the face in a store parking lot. Her son had thrown a fit because his mother insisted that he return goods he had stolen to the store. The story gained widespread publicity. After a national backlash against the arrest of the mother, the charges were eventually dropped.

This boy certainly deserved corporal punishment for his theft and subsequent tantrum, but he shouldn't have been slapped across the face. The reason is that the human face has a unique God-given dignity. The human face is for the beatific vision, where the faithful are granted the blessing to see God Himself, face-to-face.[63] In Scripture, for God's face to shine upon us is a supreme blessing.[64] Conversely, for God to turn His back on anyone is a sign of divine judgment.[65]

Following the divine pattern for blessing and for discipline, the forehead should be the place fathers make the sign of the cross and bless their children, and they should use only the rear for discipline.

What about time outs?

"Time out" can be an appropriate form of discipline for the goal of gaining compliance, but it should not replace corporal punishment in instances where harm has been intentionally done to others, or for willful insubordination. Dr. Richard Cross wisely discerns that "time outs" simply teach children that bad behavior is "non-productive to their own welfare."[66] They fail to teach a child about the debt of justice owed for bad behavior and the harm done to others.

Time outs are totally ineffective if the child is sent to a bedroom loaded with electronic games and gadgets. Such a "time out" is nothing more than an entertainment break for bad behavior.

What about lock outs?

When they are mad, have misbehaved, and especially when a spanking may be on the way, younger children might engage in a voluntary "time out" by locking their bedroom doors. Shouting threats through a locked door usually escalates a situation that needs de-escalation. I found the best way to deal with "lock out" situations during early childhood is with Dad's midnight lock repair: just install a non-locking handle until this phase passes.

The repercussions and the rewards

If you fail to set proper limits and do not consistently discipline during childhood, you'll find that your children are a frequent source of frustration. You'll look for opportunities to ship them off to some activity, so someone else will have to deal with them. By the time undisciplined children reach their teens, their parents are heartbroken, miserable, and at a loss as to what to do to change the situation.

Conversely, if with parental unity you discipline – early, consistently, lovingly, and without anger, alcohol, or abuse – then you will be rewarded with a great relationship with your children. They'll respect God, you, and other adult leaders. You'll enjoy being with them and taking them places with you. You'll want to have more children. Plus, when you father wisely during their childhood, you might even survive their teen years.

CHAPTER TEN

Fathering Sons & Fathering Daughters

In the first half of this chapter we'll cover the task of fathering sons through the transition years from boyhood to manhood. We'll devote the second half of the chapter to fathering daughters.

Boys, unlike girls, need to go through a special developmental stage for their masculinity to mature into authentic manhood.

It takes a man to convey and confirm masculinity to a boy. It doesn't come via auto pilot. It doesn't come from the most committed and talented mother, or female teacher. Therefore, it is essential for a father to be actively involved in his son's life throughout this stage of development.

Dad, let me repeat this: It takes a man (*you*, especially) to help a boy develop his masculinity. I wrote this in *The ABCs of Choosing a Good Husband*:

A young boy is naturally drawn into a close attachment to his mother. Being a "mama's boy" under seven years of age is fine and healthy. And yet for a boy to mature fully in his masculinity, he needs to "detach" from Mom and form a closer attachment with his father throughout older boyhood and adolescence.

A boy matures into manhood through this close identification with his father. Once a young man has fully matured in this way, he's ready for a close reattachment to a woman – his wife. But it's extremely difficult for a boy to mature in his masculinity without the presence of a father.[67]

Don't let yourself be absorbed by your career, sports, and hobbies apart from your sons. You've got to be with your sons in order to share your manhood with them. Expensive toys and electronic gadgets will not fill this void. It takes *you* to lead your son into his manhood.

What happens to boys when they don't have men to help them mature?

When boys don't have men to help them mature, they often develop substitutes for manhood: both hoods and homosexuals are usually those who don't successfully make the transition to manhood. "Macho" guys feel forced to assert their pseudo-masculinity, when in fact they are internally plagued by a deficiency of real manhood. Homosexuality and gender confusion also stem from the failure to make the successful transition from boyhood to manhood. Homosexuality is an increasingly common phenomenon among Catholic youth.

What should Catholic parents of a homosexual or gender confused child do? The last thing I would advise is heeding the document, *Always Our Children*.[68] I also advise keeping your children far from anyone or anything associated with the National Association of Catholic Diocesan Lesbian and Gay Ministries (NACDLGM).

Homosexuality and gender confusion are serious problems, requiring solid psychological advice, like that of Dr. Joseph Nicolosi and The Catholic Medical Association, and the National Association for Research and Therapy of Homosexuality (NARTH).[69] Dr. Nicolosi, who has spoken with hundreds of homosexual men over the past fifteen years, says, "I have never met a single homosexual man who said he had a close, loving, and respectful relationship with his father."[70]

Easy things you can do to help your son develop his masculinity

Once, when Dr. Nicolosi was a guest on my radio show, we received a call from a concerned mother about her son's masculine development. Dr. Nicolosi asked her, "How is your son's relationship with his father?" She said, "Oh, it's great. They're buddies, they play sports together all the time, and they hunt and fish together." Dr. Nicolosi said, "Everything's okay, there will be no problems." The mother, not entirely convinced, went on to voice additional concerns, but Dr. Nicolosi interrupted her and confidently predicted that this boy will turn out just fine, thanks to his relationship with his father.

So how do dads raise well-adjusted sons in our gender-confused and lack-of-genuine-manhood culture? In a nutshell: he needs to have extensive contact with his sons and share his manhood with them during the transition years. He accomplishes this through things like working with them, playing sports together, hunting, fishing, and any of the other hundreds of ways guys have lots of fun.

By sharing your life with your sons, you share your manhood with them. It is a priceless gift.

Strength training for your sons

Sons need encouragement from their fathers to develop their physical strength. God gave men strength, and it should be developed without turning a good thing into an obsession. Strengthening self-control must coincide with the development of physical strength. Wrestling with your sons is one way to teach your sons how to observe limits in the use of physical strength.

The discouragement of all aggressiveness by effeminate Christianity is a huge mistake, and a turn-off for adolescent boys. Rather than denying strength and aggressiveness in boys, wise fathers will teach their sons how to direct these energies for good. Organized sports are effective in teaching boys how to channel their strength, control aggressiveness, and focus their energy for achievement.

Before he became president, Teddy Roosevelt taught Sunday School. One Sunday, a boy came to his class with rumpled clothing and a black eye. The boy explained that a bigger boy had been picking on his sister, so he fought the bully. Teddy Roosevelt affirmed the boy's virtuous defense of his sister and gave him a dollar. The future president's act was too much for his church, so they let him go as a teacher.

Soft, effeminate, non-confrontational Christianity is a stench in the nostrils of normal men. If a young man cannot connect his masculinity with his faith, then he'll abandon it at the first opportunity. This doesn't have to happen, since courageous self-sacrifice is at the heart of masculine spirituality. Today, I wouldn't depend on many Sunday Schools and CCD classes to teach such virtues to boys.[71]

Fathers need to teach their sons that real men always treat women with respect. A man's physical strength is always used to assist and to defend women, never to strike or harm them. Teach them that retaliating for a personal insult is not necessary, but that defending the weak is virtuous.

The war for purity

The ultimate battle engaging Christian men in the twenty-first century is the war for purity. This is a life and death fight, requiring strong and virtuous fathers and sons.

Pornography is like a contagious virus passed on from father to son. It's a tragic sin, where sons follow their father's footsteps to eternal torment. I recently spoke with a man struggling with a pornography addiction that he picked up from his father. As he was going through his deceased grandfather's belongings, this man was shocked to discover that his father's porn addiction had begun with his grandfather.

Pornography is a plague on a family legacy. It needs to stop before it contaminates multiple generations of your family.

How to help your sons win the war for purity

One of the best ways to do moral "strength training" with your sons is by memorizing Scripture. These internalized verses serve as a shield guarding the mind. The Bible asks and answers the question, "How can a young man keep his way pure? By guarding it according to thy word" (Psalm 119:9).

You need to memorize Scripture along with your sons in order to ensure that they will actually accomplish it.

Couch potatoes don't win the war for purity

Couch potatoes will never get in shape, no matter how many junk products they order from infomercials on TV promising instant results. Likewise, reading this or any other book will not get you ready for spiritual warfare. You and your sons need to get into spiritual shape. You need to develop a strong shield of protection for your minds. Scripture memory doesn't come without effort, but it will give you and your sons a strong defense. At unpredictable moments of temptation, the Holy Spirit will activate a memorized verse that can guard your soul, or your son's soul.

Unfortunately, about nine out of ten men reading this book will not follow this recommendation with action. I've dealt with hundreds of men and families struggling with pornography addiction. I can say with confidence that the problem is infinitely easier to prevent than to cure. Therefore, take action and begin Scripture memory. You'll help keep your sons on the winning side in the war for purity.

Permit me to be blunt. If I had not memorized Scripture and created a scriptural shield for my mind, I would have probably plunged myself into sexual sin without recovery. I don't believe that I could have maintained my Christian morals without a strong scriptural shield for my mind.

You and your sons need a scriptural shield for the mind in order to survive today's widespread sexual license and readily available pornography, degenerate TV, movies, and music.

Basic equipment for spiritual "strength training"

Get off the couch and start your Scripture memory workouts with your sons. Gather a few dozen relevant Scriptures and make some Scripture memory cards.[72] Scripture memory with your sons is spiritual strength training to win the war for purity.

Fathering Daughters

I was recently asked to share some tips about fathering daughters. I replied, "I only have six daughters, but when I figure out something I'll let you know." Face it, all women, even our daughters, are somewhat of a mystery to us men. I'm certainly not the world's expert. Nevertheless, here are a few insights to help you father your daughters.

The father as the first "other" person

In many ways, a mother and daughter are "one." They share the same gender and they share a profound oneness during pregnancy. There is also the close mother and baby bond during the nursing years. Unlike boys, girls do not require the separation from mom that boys do during their sexual differentiation.

While mother and daughter share a "oneness" with each other, the father is the first "other person" in a girl's life. Throughout her life, his job is to introduce her to the world outside the family.

Covenant keeping: the key to fathering daughters

Since her father is the first man in a girl's life, he is the one who will form her entire conception of the world of men. Thus, the single most important thing you can do for your daughter is to love your wife in word and deed, stay married, and develop a strong marital relationship.

A father who divorces his wife saddles his daughter with an extremely tough obstacle to overcome. A deep sense of abandonment is felt by a daughter whose father divorces his wife. How can she ever trust men, when the first and most important man in her life abandoned her?

Her sense of father-loss through a divorce during childhood will not be limited to her early years. The father-loss will resurrect with a vengeance as she enters her courting years. How can she trust a husband to pledge lifelong fidelity when her father didn't?

We've already devoted a chapter to covenant keeping as the foundation of fatherhood. Thus, this key insight into fathering daughters isn't something new or different, but something that takes on an even higher importance.

Gentlemen, let me state this as directly as possible: Don't divorce your wife, or get involved in an affair. You'll harm your daughter by distorting her image of men. You'll leave lifelong scars on her heart. Sure, if you leave your wife some tribunal may give you an annulment so you can remarry someone else, but your annulment will not change the lasting harm done to your daughter.

If you are in an unhappy marriage, there is a high probability that it can become a happy one. Help is available – provided you don't get involved in an affair.[73] Men in unhappy marriages often end up with a girlfriend. Affairs are the surest way to destroy your marriage – and, subsequently, your daughter. So don't do it.

Spending time with daughters while they are young

In Chapter Two, we discussed the importance of a father spending lots of time with his children while they are young. This fatherhood time principle takes on added importance with daughters. The prime opportunities for impacting your daughters go by faster than for your sons. Let me explain.

A guy can wake up his young daughters on Saturday morning and ask, "Who wants to go to Home Depot?" Of course, everybody wants to go with Dad to Home Depot. Young girls and boys love doing anything with Dad on Saturday. Beware, guys – this changes. Your opportunities for sharing activities with your daughter diminish as she gets older and starts developing her feminine interests.

Quicker than you can imagine, she will be more interested in shoe-shopping at the mall than going with you to Home Depot. Unless you enjoy shoe-shopping, there is going to be a natural divergence between many (not all) of your interests and hers. The lesson to be learned is to maximize the opportunities during the early years, when she wants to do everything you are doing. As much as possible share your work, your errands, your hobbies, your sports, and your interests with her.

Teaching modesty

It's not easy to teach modesty, since every girl wants to dress in a way to fit in with her peers. If the primary socialization of your daughter is from her peers, then peer pressure may outweigh your standards of modesty.

Even if you and your wife have tried to be the primary socializing agents for your daughter, modesty can become a tense issue. Prudence needs to be exercised so that you don't seem rigidly strict, causing her to overreact once she leaves home for college, or moves out on her own. Unfortunately, the decadent level of immodesty in contemporary fashions makes even the reasonable requests of parents seem extreme.

Women today can't determine a standard for modesty from what others are wearing, since the standards have eroded so drastically. Many sincere Christian girls and women falsely imagine that they are dressing modestly, based upon their comparison of themselves with others. A mistake many Christian girls and women make is thinking that, as long as clothing covers the body, they are practicing modesty. They forget that clothes that cling too closely are also a grave offense to modesty.

Fathers can help their daughters understand how men are prone to sexual temptation through the eye (Matthew 5:28-29). Give them a man's perspective on what fashions are too revealing.

Before my daughters embarked on their first independent clothes shopping trip, I said, "Don't buy anything that you would be embarrassed by if the Blessed Virgin Mary were standing behind you in the checkout line." I soon forgot having ever said this, but I later discovered that my daughters didn't. Everyone needs to remember the warning at Fatima: "Certain fashions will be introduced that will offend Our LORD very much."

Dad, you are in a good position to teach your daughter how she can attract a man who will love her as a person. Teach her that modesty will protect her from immature men capable of only superficial love. Teach her how modesty will help her find a faithful man to love her.[74]

As she gets older, warn her that immodesty, hooking up, and cohabitation leave women scarred, empty, bitter, and in a joyless string of broken relationships. In contrast, encourage her with stories of how modesty and chastity lead to happiness and lasting relationships.[75]

Dads inspiring daughters to fulfill their potential

St. Thomas More is one of Christianity's best examples of a how a father can encourage his daughters to achieve their full potential. European scholars were shocked when they read the scholarly work done by one of More's daughters. Men at that time in history didn't believe that women were capable of that level of intellectual achievement. More's daughters may have swallowed their culture's preconceived notions if he hadn't had high expectations for them.

Many girls struggle with low self-esteem, and a tendency to have low expectations for themselves. Dads can help their daughters overcome their self-imposed limitations by helping them identify their unique gifts and talents, and then by encouraging their development.

As a daughter gets older, you can help her choose an opportunity for Christian service, and find meaningful summer and part-time employment. If possible, allow her to work with you in your profession. Obviously, you do these same things for your sons, but sometimes dads neglect to do them for their daughters.

The father's "great task"

The Bible says that a man has finished a "great task" when he gives his daughter in marriage to a man of understanding (Sirach 7:25). What's the great task? Is it the two minutes it takes to walk her down the aisle and give her to her husband-to-be? Hardly. The great task is the culmination of countless 60-second teaching opportunities, where you've taught your daughter about men and marriage.

Wise fathers start during childhood to prepare their daughters for choosing a good husband. Don't just give them a book to read when they are twenty years old. Rather, you need to learn what they need to know and then teach it to your daughters in short segments. Since girls begin developing an interest in serious relationships sooner than boys, start teaching them early. Why wait until your daughter is fifteen and, in her judgment, your I.Q. has dropped fifty percent?

Our society places a low value on the demanding and invaluable role of full-time mothering. Your daughter isn't going to get much cultural reinforcement if she plans to be a stay-at-home/work-at-home mother.

You can plant seeds to help your daughter realize that her worth isn't measured by the size of her paycheck, or the size of the office that she works in. A father's encouragement is a tremendous esteem-builder for his daughters to pursue the high calling of motherhood.

Beyond gender differences are individual differences

Dads shouldn't be content just to learn some of the differences between fathering sons and daughters. Each child is unique, differing even from other same-gender siblings in personality type, temperament, interests, skills, and strengths.

For instance, younger siblings often don't like being overshadowed by older siblings. Hence, they'll want to develop their own area of achievement. For one child it might be music, for another it might be football, for another it might be track, for another it might be computers. A wise father will help each of his children detect the interests and motivations that lie within them.

If you assume that the compliant nature of your firstborn daughter will be repeated in your other daughters, then you may be shocked to learn that there is such a thing as a strong-willed daughter. Sons and daughters differ one from another. Therefore, a father needs to know each of his children individually, and must try to help each child build on his or her strengths, abilities, and interests.

CHAPTER ELEVEN

Work, Adventure, and Faith

The fundamental goal for a Christian father is to see his children enjoy eternal life with him in heaven. This is the essence of building your family legacy. Since faith is necessary for salvation and eternal life, the most important legacy you can leave your children is a legacy of faith – one so strong that it will endure for generations.

How does a father build an enduring legacy of faith? It is not built using a classroom-alone strategy, dependent upon forty-five minutes of weekly instruction by a teacher who barely knows your children. A classroom-alone strategy taps only five percent of faith-building potential.

Many Catholics wonder why children can go through twelve years of Catholic school, or years of faith formation, and end up knowing practically nothing about the Faith. Reasons for this include teachers weak in their own faith and the use of defective curricula. Yet a frequently overlooked cause of faith-deficient children is a weak relational bond between teacher and students.

You'll add strength to your legacy of faith by heeding two fatherhood/faith-building strategies:

① The strength of the faith you convey to your children is directly related to the strength of your relationship with your children.

② Men primarily build relationships through shared activities.

Therefore, if you want to build a strong legacy of faith in your family, then multiply and deepen shared activities with your children. This will result in a strong relational bond with them.

Most men don't build relationships through sitting in a circle and talking. Rather, they excel at building relationships through doing things together. A father is at his best if he adopts a shared activity as a critical step in his plan to build a legacy of faith.

The relationships built through these activities are like a bridge that the Faith crosses over to the hearts of your children. The stronger the bridge, the stronger the faith conveyed. As you build these bonds, a modest amount of faith sharing with your children will have a profound and enduring effect.

I can't emphasize strongly enough the importance of implementing this simple strategy. I've used it to build a successful children's ministry, two youth ministries, and in my own family. It works supremely well, and you will have fun in the process. If you are a classroom religion teacher, then be sure to achieve lasting influence by engaging in some type of shared activity with your students outside of the classroom.

Most fathers can't envision themselves as successful teachers of the Faith, because they think effective teaching is like leading a classroom discussion. In reality, if you regularly go fishing, play sports, and work together with your kids, then you've already accomplished seventy-five percent of the teaching task; that is, you've already built the strong relational bridge that the Faith crosses.

Building bridges through work

From the dawn of civilization until the nineteenth century, working together was the primary way fathers built bonds with their children. Before the Industrial Revolution, workplace and home were frequently the same place for fathers, whether on a family farm or in a cottage industry. All of this has changed. Today, children often have little idea of what their fathers do at work.

Working side-by-side with your children is a vital component of fathering, yet it is commonly neglected today. Jesus never set foot in a seminary or a rabbinic school. His ministerial training took place in St. Joseph's workshop. Jesus watched St. Joseph work, and then joined him in those tasks. The carpenter's shop was Jesus' preparation for His three-year public ministry.

In St. John's Gospel, we see Jesus ministering with His Heavenly Father according to the father/son paradigm that He learned in the carpenter's shop:

> Jesus said to them, "Truly, truly, I say to you, the Son can do nothing of his own accord, but only what he sees the Father doing; for whatever he does, that the Son does likewise. For the Father loves the Son, and shows him all that he himself is doing; and greater works than these will he show him, that you may marvel" (John 5:19-20).

The carpenter's shop pattern is for today

St. Joseph is the world's best model of earthly fatherhood. Christian fathers know that they should look to St. Joseph for the pattern of their own fatherhood. So why do we often neglect the carpenter's shop model for our own fatherhood? The model of fathers and sons (and daughters) working together has been destroyed by modern economic life.

The carpenter's shop isn't just a nice story from biblical times; it is the timeless pattern for fathering with a lasting legacy. Wise fathers will plan and take necessary steps to recover the carpenter's shop pattern for their own families. Don't give up on the idea because it is hard to do in today's world. Gather some steam and do it.

Here are some examples of work-with-your-kids ideas:

- If your job or business allows your children to work with you, do it

- If you are able, purchase a home with property around it, requiring you and your children to work together in order to maintain it

- Start a home-based business, or a Saturday-only business, that allows you and your children to work together. Use caution in selecting a home-based business, since most of the heavily-marketed home-based businesses are losers or pyramid schemes. Yet there are many good opportunities[76]

- Volunteer for service projects that allow families (not just youth groups) to work together

- Take a child with you on business trips

- Buy a small farm[77]

Don't allow our abnormal times to separate one hundred percent of your work life from your children. Be creative, and determine to find ways to work with your children. It is one of the primary ways dads build a relational bridge with their children.

Don't give your children everything – allow them to work

Rather than giving your children everything, it is better to allow them to work and earn money for their purchases. Hard work builds discipline and virtue. In contrast, a life of prosperous ease is an environment for harmful passions and vices to grow.

Many wonder why so many Catholic children from prosperous yet pious families fall away from the Faith. I believe that too much prosperous ease is a major unrecognized cause. *The Truth and Meaning of Human Sexuality*, from the Pontifical Council for the Family, warns:

> An undisciplined or spoiled child is inclined toward a certain immaturity and moral weakness in future years because chastity is difficult to maintain if a person develops selfish or disordered habits.[78]

In a similar vein, Ezekiel proclaims God's analysis of the causes for Sodom's slide into debauchery:

> Behold, this was the guilt of your sister Sodom: she and her daughters had pride, surfeit of food, and prosperous ease, but did not aid the poor and needy. They were haughty, and did abominable things before me; therefore I removed them, when I saw it (Ezekiel 16:49-50).

I'm not a socialist or an anti-business type of person, but prosperous ease is something potentially harmful to children in environments of middle-class and upper middle-class lifestyles. When Christians are outwardly attacked and resist, they become much stronger. Unfortunately, the seductions born of prosperity are much more difficult to resist, and even to detect. Pope Leo XIII warned that virtue is lulled to sleep by a soft, delicate, and pleasure-seeking life.[79]

Too much money and "stuff" chokes the life of grace in the hearts of both children and adults. If your family is living the average middle-class American lifestyle, then you are experiencing levels of prosperity unknown in all of human history. American children ages four to twelve spend $35 billion annually, and get about seventy new toys per year.[80] They possess more than any generation in history.

Giving your children (and teens) too much is one of the biggest mistakes that parents make. Excessive materialism brings about inner poverty and emptiness. Children living with a large amount of material goods experience depression at three times the normal levels, have lower self-esteem, have higher rates of substance abuse and worse relationships with parents. Overindulgence chokes God's Word, and creates selfish and dissatisfied children. All of us, myself included, need to be vigilant in resisting the allure of consumerism.

Hard, sweaty work and lack of abundance were the consequences of Adam's original sin, as announced by God in the Garden of Eden. These consequences weren't indiscriminate or cruel punishments pronounced against Adam. A closer look reveals that they were gracious disciplines, meant to keep sinful tendencies from multiplying. Hard work is an overlooked way to build virtue and restrain those vices fueled by prosperous ease. Family work is also one of the primary ways to build strong bonds with your children.

Building bonds through fun and adventure

Another way dads build strong relational bonds with their children is through sharing fun and adventure.

Highly religious fathers tend to neglect fun and adventure in life. As their children get older, these dads wonder why their children end up rejecting them and their faith. Stories abound in literature about sons rejecting the faith of their stern and joyless New England Calvinist fathers. Catholic men aren't excluded from making this tragic mistake. Don't try to make your home into a strict monastery. The Faith should be central in your family, but not to the exclusion of enjoyment in life.

Devout believers face the perennial problem of faithlessness in the second generation. One cause for failing to reach the second generation is that parents who have come to experience a strong union with Christ expect their children to automatically experience the same. Rarely is this the case. Such parents must remember to lighten up, and link up with their children by having fun and adventure with them. Building closeness through fun and adventure will make it much easier for the Faith to be shared between generations.

The English martyr, St. Thomas More, was utterly serious in his practice of the Faith. Nevertheless, More kept joy alive in his family with his warm sense of humor. He even kept a monkey as a household pet, in order to entertain his family. If you are ever tempted to squeeze fun and enjoyment out of your family life, just remember More's monkey!

There are dozens of ways to build strong relational bonds with your children through fun and adventure. Here are just a few examples of what you can do:

- Fishing
- Hunting and skeet shooting
- Sports of all types
- ATVs and dirt-biking
- Canoeing & kayaking
- Mountain biking
- Surfing
- White-water rafting
- Hiking and camping
- Snorkeling & skin diving
- Water-skiing & snow-skiing
- Paintball

One of the things I enjoy doing with my children is off-road dirt-biking. When I got the dirt bikes a close friend said, "You are the last person on earth that I thought would buy dirt bikes." Translated, this remark means, "You are religious, therefore I thought you wouldn't enjoy wild-and-crazy fun."

Boys, especially, seem to enjoy adrenaline-producing activities. It's great for a dad to share these activities with his sons; it also keeps the boys from getting injured when they get too carried away with the fun.

Amusement parks are fun places to take your kids to, but I don't think that they have the same potential to build the relational bond as do sports and more nature-based outside activities.

In summary, in order to start one of the world's best religious educations, do the following: shoot, fish, eat, work, play, ride in the truck, and have lots of fun. Not too complicated. Remember to engage in some slightly risk-taking fun with them – religious dads sometimes forget this. My attorney advises me against giving specific recommendations for this risk-taking component of fathering, but I'm sure you can come up with something!

Using your bridge to build a legacy of faith

As you build and maintain your relational bridge with your children, your efforts at sharing the Faith will have staying power. Use this strategy to build a legacy of faith even in an age when millions of Catholic youth cease practicing their faith before they leave their teen years. You'll have success with the faith-building plan in the next chapter if you remember to couple it with relational bridge-building through work, adventure, fun, and sports.

CHAPTER TWELVE

Building a Legacy of Faith

In past generations, parents may have gotten by depending solely upon religious education programs (CCD) and Catholic schools for their children's faith formation. Today, countless parents are discovering too late that something else besides classroom instruction is needed for the Faith to survive.

Good Catholic schools and solid religious education programs are valuable, but you should not depend upon them alone for the eternal welfare of your children. Every good religion teacher knows the value of formation in the home.

Family catechesis is not optional

John Paul II emphasized that family faith formation is necessary in cultures that are experiencing widespread secularism:

> Family catechesis therefore precedes, accompanies and enriches all other forms of catechesis. Furthermore, in places where widespread unbelief or invasive secularism makes real religious growth practically impossible, "the Church of the home" remains the one place where children and young people can receive an authentic catechesis. Thus there cannot be too great an effort on the part of Christian parents to prepare for this ministry of being their own children's catechists and to carry it out with tireless zeal.[81]

This "Church of the home" catechetical strategy needs to be taken one step further if the culture gets really bad (like ours). What type of catechesis will allow faith and morals to survive when a society becomes a cultural sewer? Instruction by fathers is the only kind of catechesis that will succeed in such an environment.

Genesis 18 describes Sodom and Gomorrah, the wicked cultural environment adjacent to where Abraham lived. Despite the disintegrating surrounding society, God promised to bless Abraham with an enduring legacy of faith, knowing that Abraham would personally instruct his children in "the way of the LORD."

> Abraham shall become a great and mighty nation, and all the nations of the earth shall bless themselves by him ... for I have chosen him, that he may charge his children and his household after him to keep the way of the LORD by doing righteousness and justice; so that the LORD may bring to Abraham what he has promised him (Genesis 18:18-19).

The day is past when a dad can dump all of the children's religious instruction on his wife's shoulders and still expect his sons and daughters to end up being faithful practicing Christians. St. Paul, writing in the context of family and married life, singles out fathers for the faith formation of their children. "Fathers ... bring them up in the discipline and instruction of the LORD" (Ephesians 6:4). Sure, mothers must be involved, but dads can't go AWOL when it comes to religious instruction.

Dads: the cure for church dropout

Millions of Catholic children grow up and fall away from regular church attendance. Such willful neglect of Sunday worship is a violation of the Third Commandment and a mortal sin. In the United States it is estimated that only thirteen percent of eighteen-to twenty-nine-year-olds believe that they must always obey the pope's formal teachings.[82] In England, ninety-two percent of Catholic young people stop practicing their religion when they leave school.[83] In

Australia, official Church figures report that ninety-five percent of teens who attend Catholic schools leave the Church.[84]

The cure for this massive church dropout is Dad. Research shows that if a father attends church regularly, he conveys a lasting lesson to his children. A Swiss study asked the question, "What causes a person's faith to carry through from childhood to adult religious belief and practice?"[85] The study found that the one overwhelming critical factor is the religious practice of the father. Dads determine the church habits of their children, and thus, to a significant degree, their eternal destiny.

Can't mom also do this? Shockingly, the study reported that "If a father does not go to church, no matter how faithful his wife's devotions, only one child in fifty will become a regular worshipper." Yet, "If a father does go regularly, regardless of the practice of the mother, between two-thirds and three-quarters of their children will become churchgoers (regular and irregular)."[86]

Therefore, your first step in building a lasting faith legacy is to attend church regularly.

Be a living model of moral absolutes

The second step in building a legacy of faith is to be a living model of moral absolutes. The moral system that children today are adopting is called relativism. It is moral decision-making based upon: what seems right to me, what seems right in a particular situation, what friends think is right, what feels right. Such self-centered patterns of moral decision-making are just like the temptation that Satan gave to Eve in the Garden of Eden. The master of deception said, "Your eyes will be opened, and you will be like God, knowing good and evil" (Genesis 3:5).

Big trouble follows when we pretend that we are like God, capable of determining good and evil. It is God's prerogative to determine and to declare good and evil. Our job is to obey, not to define morality. Yet values clarification (i.e., self-determination of right from wrong) is the system of morality taught in drug prevention programs, and in most classroom sex education curricula; it is endlessly portrayed in the media, and relentlessly brainwashed into students from kindergarten to Ph.D seminars. You'll even find it in countless Catholic youth programs, and in many Catholic schools. I even encountered it in a diocesan diaconal training program.

Children growing up in the toxic atmosphere of moral relativism may not seem much different from those growing up with moral absolutes. There may be no visible evidence of harm, even as these children have the foundation for living a moral life eroded from underneath them. When children without moral absolutes hit their teen years, however, all hell can break loose with their moral behavior. Trying to communicate morality to such a teen can seem like talking to someone from another galaxy.

Lack of moral absolutes is the root of immoral behavior. For example, author Josh McDowell, drawing upon the research of George Barna, reports that youth without moral absolutes are four times more likely to approve of premarital intercourse than those with them.[87]

Your goal should be to teach moral absolutes to your children. You need to tell them that certain things are right for all people, at all times, and in all situations. Besides keeping your children in educational settings free from moral relativism, they need, above all, your consistent living example.

Enoch: a father walking with God

Your children need to see you make your decisions and consistently live all of your life in conformity to the moral law. When a father does this, the Bible calls it "walking with God." A man who walks with God in conformity with moral absolutes is on the road to building a lasting legacy of faith.

The Bible says that after Enoch became the father of Methuselah, he began "walking with God" in the midst of a corrupt culture. As a reward for Enoch's consistent walk, God took him directly into heaven (Genesis 5:22-24).

Surrounded by a world that has plunged headlong into moral eclipse, many fathers might despair of their own children remaining faithful Christians. Be encouraged by the fruit of Enoch's walk with God. It had trans-generational effects.

Enoch's great-grandson

When the ancient world had reached the moral degeneracy terminal point, we meet Enoch's great-grandson: Noah. What does the Bible say about Noah?

"Noah was a righteous man, blameless in his generation; Noah walked with God" (Genesis 6:9). In a world where literally everyone was corrupt and wicked, Noah was walking with God, and thus he saved his family from the destruction of the Flood.

Enoch's walk with God was a potent family legacy inherited by Noah that enabled his faith to survive in the worst possible cultural context. Your walk with God has the same potential.

"You shall not do as they do"

Before the children of Israel entered the Promised Land occupied by morally corrupt peoples, God warned them through Moses not to follow the example of the Canaanite culture that they were entering, or the Egyptian culture they were leaving.

You shall not do as they do in the land of Egypt, where you dwelt, and you shall not do as they do in the land of Canaan, to which I am bringing you. You shall not walk in their statutes. You shall do my ordinances and keep my statutes and walk in them. I am the LORD your God (Leviticus 18:3-4).

A father needs to give the same exhortation to his children, encouraging them to follow God and not the crowd. But for a dad's exhortation to have impact and staying power, it needs to be coupled with his personal example: walking with God and not succumbing to the pitfalls of the surrounding degenerate culture.

God's Word and a father's voice

A vital ingredient in building a legacy of faith is making sure that your children hear God's Word through your voice. This isn't an option. In Psalm 78 God commands fathers to speak his Word to their children.

> I will open my mouth in a parable; I will utter dark sayings from of old, (3) things that we have heard and known, that our fathers have told us. (4) We will not hide them from their children, but tell to the coming generation the glorious deeds of the LORD, and his might, and the wonders which he has wrought. (5) He established a testimony in Jacob, and appointed a law in Israel, which he commanded our fathers to teach to their children; (6) that the next generation might know them, the children yet unborn, and arise and tell them to their children, (7) so that they should set their hope in God, and not forget the works of God, but keep his commandments; (8) and that they should not be like their fathers, a stubborn and rebellious generation, a generation whose heart was not steadfast, whose spirit was not faithful to God.

Notice that God singles out fathers. You cannot subcontract this fatherly responsibility to a school or to a religious educator. Nor should you expect your wife to do all the religious education of your children.

There are two lasting benefits that arise when a father fulfills the duty of teaching his children. First, fatherly instruction prevents faith washout (verses 7 and 8 above). Children taught by their dads are not inclined to be rebellious, lack steadfastness, or be unfaithful toward God. Classroom instruction alone can't provide these assurances.

The second benefit, highlighted in verse 6 above, is that you establish a family pattern that your sons and the husbands of your daughters will follow in teaching your grandchildren. Your grandsons will continue what you began by teaching your great-grandchildren. A few words regularly spoken about the Faith by a father to his children are potent enough to last for generations.

How does a father instruct his family in Scripture?

After your family's evening meal, take five minutes to read Scripture. There's no need to overdo it. A paragraph is long enough if you have young children, or as much as an entire chapter as your children get older. It's a good idea for the father to start the Bible reading. In our family we usually let everyone old enough to read take turns reading the passage.

You can make all or a portion of the daily Mass readings your family's readings, or you can simply go through various books of the Bible. The four Gospels, the Psalms, Proverbs, and a few epistles (like Galatians, Ephesians, and Philippians) are good starting places.

After reading the passage, the father can ask a few questions pertaining to the text and answer any questions that the kids have about the text. There are several good Bible study options that will assist you in this responsibility.[88]

Men's study groups seem to be always looking for some good study material. I suggest that a men's small group study a book of the Bible in a way that prepares fathers for leading discussions on the same book in their homes. I can't think of a higher purpose for a men's study group.

Promise of a legacy of faith to parents speaking words of Scripture

Just how potent is it when fathers and mothers speak God's words to their children? Note carefully the encouraging multi-generational blessing God promises to such families.

> And as for me, this is my covenant with them, says the LORD: my spirit which is upon you, and my words which I have put in your mouth, shall not depart out of your mouth, or out of the mouth of your children, or out of the mouth of your children's children, says the LORD, from this time forth and for evermore (Isaiah 59:21).

Training children for a lifetime of worship

Your goal in training children for worship is to prepare them for a lifetime of Mass attendance and participation. The principle to use in training your children for worship comes from Proverbs 22:6: "Train up a child in the way he should go, and when he is old he will not depart from it." Application of the Proverbs 22:6 principle means that you'll want to start this type of training in early childhood so that it will last a lifetime.

Applying this principle will challenge some common assumptions about children and Mass. I think that children's Masses, though well intended, are a mistake. When children are young, they are at their maximum adaptability. They permanently absorb whatever they are introduced to. Why give them a dumbed-down children's liturgy and homily, and then require them to adapt to an adult liturgy when they are older and less adaptable?

The foundation for the godly formation of your children includes the "fear of the LORD." This isn't being afraid of God; it means a profound reverential awe for God. Children don't need to immediately understand every word and liturgical act, but they do need to see a profoundly reverent liturgy that they'll never outgrow.

A casual, user-friendly children's Mass often lacks the reverence and mystery that draws the child deeply into the worship of God. The more contemporary the style of the liturgy, the sooner it will become obsolete, irrelevant, outgrown, and cast underfoot.

Another mistake is taking children out of Mass during the homily. It is a blessing for families to be united for the entire Mass. Modern life weakens families by separating family members most of the week. The last thing families need is to be separated from each other during Mass. Children can learn to sit quietly through a homily. Taking them out robs them of the opportunity to learn how to listen to a sermon during the ages of maximum adaptability. The entire liturgy of the Mass can and needs to be rooted in children from the youngest ages. Besides, children often surprise their parents by repeating something the priest said in his homily that the parents didn't think was heard or understood by the child.

Reverent liturgies are the best liturgies

I know it is a surprise to many, but young families are flocking to parishes offering reverent liturgies, including parishes offering the Latin Mass (done with the local bishop's approval). Other families are discovering the beauty, mystery, and awe in the centuries-old Byzantine Catholic liturgy. Young parents who were force-fed trendy liturgies in their youth are now turning to more timeless forms of worship.

A reverent liturgy exudes the holiness of God, and intuitively conveys a sense of His special presence. Balloons, banners, skits, and other hoopla are liturgical chaff. Children need exposure to a reverent liturgy fitting for the worship of the thrice-holy God.

Architecture teaches children reverence for God

My six-year-old son ran ahead of us, and peeked in the front door of Sacred Heart Church in downtown Tampa. With wide eyes he spun around and shouted, "Wow!"

What John had seen was a beautifully decorated sanctuary – the kind built in an era when the majestic transcendence of God was boldly manifested in architecture. Most of the churches we had attended in Florida were newer ones, whose architecture emphasized the immanence (closeness) of God.

Once, while we were still Protestants, I attended a pro-life rally with a few of my children at an ultra-modern Catholic church. Some time afterward, my nine-year-old daughter was trying to refresh my memory about the rally and was having a difficult time describing this particular church. Finally she said, "You know, the church that looked like the mall." I instantly remembered the church she was describing.

Back to Sacred Heart. During Mass, John's eyes scanned the majestic statues, the high altar, and the beautifully decorated gold dome. During the homily he whispered to me in an intensely inquisitive tone, "Dad, who built this place?" I answered slowly and deliberately, "Some people who think God is really great."

Teaching children reverential awe for God Almighty isn't easy, especially in a generation that has distorted the knowledge of God with too many liturgical innovations, lectors processing in jogging suits, corny hymns, a man-centered theology, and sanctuaries with mall-like architecture.

Reverence – the mother of all virtues

Dietrich von Hildebrand called reverence "the mother of all virtues ... and the basic attitude that all virtues presuppose."[89] He insisted that the knowledge of God only reveals itself to reverent minds. Therefore, teaching reverence is a necessary foundation for a solid faith, and for developing moral purity.[90]

Young children learn eighty percent by the eye and twenty percent by the ear. You can start teaching reverence to your children through simple acts, such as the devout attitude reflected in your genuflection, the careful manner in which you make the Sign of the Cross, and your posture at Mass. It's also important for them to see liturgy and architecture that reflects the glory of God.

On a family vacation, why not go a little out of your way to attend Mass at one of the older, more majestic churches that can be found in most parts of the country? It is also worth the drive to attend a parish where reverence is clearly demonstrated in the liturgy.

Teaching reverential awe is foundational to the knowledge of God and preparatory for an awakening of His greatness.

Children's missals and Cheerios

Besides influencing the important decision of the type of Mass you want to attend with your children, the Proverbs 22:6 principle can also be used for less important decisions.

I do think children's missals are a good idea. The picture missal teaches children to follow along with the Mass and keeps their attention focused. It introduces them to a behavior, i.e., using a missal, that they can use lifelong.

What about the near-universal practice of letting children snack on Cheerios to keep them quiet during Mass? Though the Cheerios question isn't a big deal, it is illustrative of ways to apply Proverbs 22:6. Why would you want to initiate a behavior (snacking during Mass) that you are going to have to stop in the future? There are much better ways to keep children behaved during Mass.

How to teach your children to sit through Mass

Most parents try to teach their children to sit through Mass by struggling with them for sixty minutes each week, resulting in months of embarrassing moments in church. There is a far easier way to do this.

I recommend taking five minutes per day for a few weeks, in order to accomplish what otherwise takes months, or even a few years. Here is how it works.

Have a family prayer time with your young children that doesn't exceed five minutes. Mom holds the newborn and allows him to nurse if necessary. Dad holds the toddler on his lap using my anti-escape hold.

Here's how to do the anti-escape hold:

1. Place the child on your left leg facing forward

2. Put your right arm across his right leg and with your right hand grasp your left thigh

3. Reach your left arm across the mid-section of your child and grasp your right arm just beneath the elbow

4. Switch knees and arms after standing for a reading or prayer

Your child can wiggle, but can't escape this hold. Any pressure required to keep him in the hold is applied to your limbs and not his. As you sit down for a few minutes for family prayer, place the child on your lap as I've described. If he attempts to move away and can't, he's liable to raise his voice a few decibels. Just ignore the noise and calmly hold him. When your prayer time is finished, just let him get down. After a few days (or a few weeks for the strong-willed and wiggle-worms) he will just quit making a fuss.

God gives rewards – why can't parents?

The Bible says that God rewards his children for doing what was expected and commanded of them. Why can't parents do the same for children who sit quietly through Mass? It's a good idea to have a special treat on Sundays, especially if you are training younger children. We used ice cream when our kids were younger. Once, during the middle of a Mass, my daughter said, "Do I get ice cream?" Her attention wasn't focused on the Mass that day, but at least she was trying hard to earn her little reward. It doesn't take too many ice cream sundaes for children to learn that it pays to be good during Mass. Rewards, or occasionally withholding them, are powerful motivators for small children. They are not only effective in training for Mass, but are useful to motivate good manners and patient behavior during shopping trips and visits to restaurants.

Using restaurants to train for sitting through Mass

Just like using your home, a wise choice of restaurants can help you train your children to sit quietly for a stretch of time. Both the home and restaurants are far less stressful environments to deal with loud crying than an otherwise quiet sanctuary.

A successful restaurant visit begins with a wise choice of where you are going to eat. When children are young, I recommend a restaurant with quick service and soft-serve ice cream. It is difficult for children to sit quietly for long stretches of time. You want them to experience a string of successes in sitting quietly for moderate periods. The fast service helps make for a successful experience. The more tired your kids are, the quicker the service you will need to provide the framework for a successful restaurant experience. The ice cream bar with all the stuff they can put on top is a magical motivator for getting good behavior at restaurants. It's their delicious reward for behaving while sitting through a meal.

Once kids learn to sit quietly at home and at restaurants, it will be much easier to get them to sit quietly through Mass. In addition, a father who makes the effort to train his children this way opens the door for countless opportunities to take his children with him – often to places other parents wouldn't dream of taking their kids.

Family prayer

It is very important that the father of the family lead his family in prayer. Mother Teresa wrote this instruction to all the St. Joseph's Covenant Keepers:

> Be sure to teach the families to pray all together – father, mother and children. For the family that prays together stays together, and if they stay together they will love one another as Jesus loves each one of them.[91]

If you are starting out with family prayer, make it your goal to be consistent. For example, if your children are young, antsy, and unaccustomed to family prayer, then you might begin by praying just a decade of the Rosary. As your children and your practice of family prayer both mature, you can extend your prayer to five decades of the Rosary.

You will find it easier to develop consistency if you have a regular time and place for family prayer. For many families, a time for prayer after the evening meal works well. Other families prefer bedtime. Whatever time your family chooses, just do it.

Finding time for family prayer

The big obstacle hindering family prayer for millions of families is their hectic schedule. Fewer than a third of all American children sit down to eat dinner with both parents on any given evening. If you're finding it difficult to gather your family, then I suggest choosing a time on Sunday and one weekday as your times for developing a pattern of family prayer. Many sports teams don't schedule Wednesday nights in deference to Protestant mid-week prayer services and youth groups. If this is the situation in your community, then make Wednesday evening (along with Sunday) the special times for your family meal, Scripture reading and prayer time.

With the frantic pace of modern life, the time for family meals and family prayer isn't going to be delivered to your front door. It is going to be up to you to carve it out of your schedule. These few special moments shared by families powerfully influence the temporal and eternal welfare of your family.

A study by the National Center on Addiction and Substance Abuse at Columbia University found that teens who regularly eat dinner with their family have half the risk of abusing drugs and alcohol. A surprising finding of this study was that eating together as a family was more predictive of good behavior than either church attendance or school grades.[92]

Family meals are important for family unity. Just remember that a family eating with the TV on is having a TV dinner, not a family meal. (The only two exceptions to this principle are when the Tampa Bay Buccaneers or the Florida Gators are playing.)

Don't go overboard

Don't become like the fanatical father I heard about, who scheduled multiple holy hours on the weekend and included his children under seven years old. Family prayer is critically important, yet dads who go overboard with this good thing are making a big mistake. Your family is a family, not a seminary or a monastery.

Take God on vacation

Don't leave God behind when you go on vacation. Take advantage of the "family together" time that a vacation gives you. It's a great family tradition to start each day of a car trip by praying the Rosary together.

Be sure to take your children with you

Many families have a horror story of leaving a child behind at a gas station, a restaurant, or at home. Usually the mistake is quickly realized, and the frightened family is peacefully reunited. Following such an incident, parents are diligent with their nose counts before heading out.

Ironically, many parents who panic over leaving a child behind for a few minutes seem unconcerned with leaving their children behind on life's greatest journey.

Our life is a spiritual pilgrimage. One of the first books I read after my Christian conversion was *Pilgrim's Progress* by John Bunyan. Though the book helped me immensely to get going in the Christian life, I've come to see a significant flaw in Bunyan's work. The pilgrim in the allegory leaves his family behind to set out on his journey to the eternal city. Yet the ideal pattern in Scripture is for families to experience salvation together.

Even very religious fathers can be so absorbed in their own pilgrimage that they neglect the salvation of their children. If you are a father, then you have the responsibility to assist in the saving of your children. When Noah was warned of the impending flood, he didn't build a kayak for the saving of himself alone. The Bible says that he constructed an ark for the saving of his household (Hebrews 11:7).

Throughout salvation history, the normative pattern of salvation envisions family members embracing the Faith together. In the Book of Acts, the Philippian jailer asked St. Paul, "What must I do to be saved?" St. Paul's timeless answer was, "Believe in the LORD Jesus, and you will be saved, you and your household" (Acts 16:31). Household salvation was a normative pattern in the first century Church. It should be the same in the twenty-first century.

As Jacob returns to the holy land in Genesis 33, he prefigures our return to dwell with Jesus Christ for eternity. As Esau sees Jacob and his family returning, he asks, "Who are these with you?" Jacob answers, "The children whom God has graciously given your servant" (Genesis 33:5). May our answer be the same when we enter the holy land of the new earth for all eternity. Salvation embracing a household doesn't just happen automatically. It takes Christian fathers doing everything in their power to shepherd their children to eternal life. For married men, this is their most important job on earth.

In a day when millions of Christians are seeking to live a purpose-filled life, fathers should place their family responsibilities at the heart of their life purpose. What is more important than having multiple generations of your family enjoying eternal life together with Christ on the transformed new earth?

Saving a life

I've had only one opportunity to save someone's physical life. It was during my teen years. I was standing on a gas dock at a marina and saw out of the corner of my eye a boat explode into flames. An inboard cruiser that had recently fueled didn't sufficiently exhaust the gas fumes after fueling. The panicked skipper jumped overboard on the leeward side of his boat, which resulted in the burning boat drifting right over him. I only had seconds to decide that this man was in serious trouble and that I needed to act. I yelled to a friend who joined me in my boat, and we sped off to rescue the terrified skipper as shooting flames burned a few feet away.

It's a rewarding experience to save someone's life, but such emergencies can't be planned or predicted. It is something that presents itself as quick as lightning and demands an instant response.

Saving your child

I believe that every one of you reading this book would jump into action to rescue your child from life-threatening physical danger. If necessary, you would risk your life. Shouldn't we be willing to do the same for our child's body and soul for all eternity?

There is really no excuse; after all, we have years of opportunities to cooperate with God in the saving of our children. It is something that we can deliberate on carefully, and take planned action. We are without excuse if we don't act.

My hope and my goal as a father, despite my failings, is to be able to answer Christ's question on the final day, "Whom do you bring with you?" with the reply, "The children whom God has graciously given your servant."

Fathering isn't an easy job in today's world, but remember that we are not in this alone. The hand of God the Father is on our shoulders as we undertake the greatest work a father can do – cooperating in the saving of his household. With the strength of God's grace, let us put our shoulders to the task of building a legacy of faith.

Prayer for a Family Legacy

O Most Holy, Almighty, and Eternal God and Father, King of Heaven and Earth, You are the Creator of all things that exist, and the Redeemer of all who place their trust in You.

You are the ever merciful and faithful God, who keeps covenant and steadfast love to a thousand generations with those who love You and keep Your commandments.

In the name of your Son, our LORD Jesus Christ, I ask You to have mercy on me and our family, and to always forgive us when we sin against You.

Keep the generations of our family from evil and bestow upon us Your Holy Spirit that we may always know, love, serve, and obey You.

Grant to each generation wisdom in the choice of vocation. Raise up men and women who will serve Your Church with holy fear and with love. Grant to those preparing for the Sacrament of Holy Matrimony wisdom and protection in the selection of a spouse.

In Your goodness, make the marriages in our family fruitful, with an abundance of godly children.

May the generations of my family be guarded and guided by Your infallible and inspired words of Holy Scripture. May You grant to them an open ear to hear and to obey both

Sacred Scripture and Sacred Tradition. May they always walk in the way of Your precepts.

May the parents, especially the fathers, teach the Faith to their children so that the next generation might know You and place their trust in You.

In Your abundant mercy and grace, grant to my family a legacy of faith unto countless generations, so that they may keep the Faith of the One, Holy, Catholic, and Apostolic Church.

O LORD and King Jesus Christ, in Your mercy hear and answer this prayer.

May Holy Mary, Saint Joseph, and all the Saints petition the LORD that my family may obtain grace and salvation from Him who lives and reigns forever.

May St. Michael and his angelic host keep them from the powers of darkness in this world, and may their guardian angels ever protect them.

Amen.[93]

ENDNOTES

---

[1] Theodore Roosevelt, *Theodore Roosevelt: An Autobiography* (New York: MacMillan, 1913, chapter IX, "Outdoors and Indoors." Available online at Bartleby.com Great Books Online, http://www. bartleby.com/55/9.html.

[2] David Blankenhorn, *Fatherless America: Confronting Our Most Urgent Social Problem* (New York: Basic Books, 1995), p. 12.

[3] Anthony Guerra, *Family Matters: The Role of Christianity in the Formation of the Western Family* (St. Paul, MN: Paragon House, 2002), p. 45.

[4] Sociologist John Robinson of the University of Maryland, *USA Today*, May 10, 1991. Keith Epstein, "How We Countered the 'Family-Time' Famine," *The Washington Post*, April 11, 1994, cited by Robert L. Maginnis in "Parents and Community Remain the Best Defense Against Drugs," Family Research Council, Washington, D.C., October 1998, p. 10.

[5] Steven L. Nock and Paul William Kingston, "Time with Children: The Impact of Couples' Work-Time Commitments," *Social Forces*, September 1, 1988, pp. 59-85, cited by Robert L. Maginnis in "Parents and Community Remain the Best Defense Against Drugs," Family Research Council, Washington, D.C., October 1998, p. 10.

[6] *Family in America Report* (The Howard Center, 934 North Main Street, Rockford, IL, 61103), June 2005, p. 4, reporting on a study by Anne Poortman entitled, "How Work Affects Divorce: The Mediating Role of Financial and Time Pressures," *Journal of Family Issues* 26 (March 2005): pp. 168-195.

[7] Maggie Gallagher, "The Importance of Being Married," chapter 6 in *The Fatherhood Movement: A Call to Action,* Wade F. Horn,

David Blankenhorn, and Mitchell B. Pearlstein, editors, (Lanham, MD: Lexington Books, 1999), p. 59, citing Frank F. Furstenberg Jr. and Andrew J. Cherlin, *Divided Families: What Happens to Children When Parents Part* (Cambridge, MA: Harvard University Press, 1991), pp. 35-36.

[8] *Father Facts*, Fourth Edition (Gaithersburg, MD: National Fatherhood Initiative, 2002), pp. 15, 46-51.

[9] Lawrence Kubie, "The Desire to Become Both Sexes," *Psychoanalytic Quarterly* 43, no. 3 (July 1974), p. 370.

[10] *Father Facts*, Fourth Edition (Gaithersburg, MD: National Fatherhood Initiative, 2002), p. 51, citing Feng, Du, Roseann Giarrusso, Vern L. Bengtson, and Nancy Frye, "Intergenerational Transmission of Marital Quality and Marital Instability," *Journal of Marriage and the Family* 61 (1999): pp. 451-463.

[11] Pope Leo XIII, *A Light in the Heavens: The Great Encyclical Letters of Pope Leo XIII* (Rockford, IL: TAN Publishers, 1995), p. 75.

[12] Maggie Gallagher and Linda J. Waite, *The Case for Marriage: Why Married People Are Happier, Healthier, and Better Off Financially* (New York: Doubleday, 2000), pp. 75, 148-149. 86% of those who rated their marriage as "unhappy" (versus "very unhappy") and yet stayed married, said five years later that their marriage was happier.

[13] See the "Saving Marriages" resources at http://familylifecenter.net/.

[14] Janet E. Smith, *Humanae Vitae: A Generation Later* (Washington, D.C.: Catholic University of America Press, 1991), pp. 127, 391. Among spouses teaching NFP with the Couple to Couple League, the divorce rate is 1.4%. It is estimated that the divorce rate for all couples using NFP may be up to three times this number, or 4.2%, which is still less than a tenth of the national divorce rate.

[15] For more detail about birth control, Natural Family Planning, and a father's attitude toward children, see James Burnham and Stephen Wood, *Christian Fatherhood: The Eight Commitments of*

St. Joseph's Covenant Keepers (Port Charlotte, FL: Family Life Center Publications, 1997), chapter 10, pp. 124-139.

[16] To learn more about Natural Family Planning, visit http://dads.org/article.asp?artId=303.

[17] For a comprehensive list of resources to help break free from a pornography habit, visit http://dads.org/strugglewithporn.asp.

[18] For selected resources to help with alcoholism see http://dads.org/article.asp?artId=337. The best book for a Christian perspective on alcoholism is Anderson Spickard and Barbara R. Thompson, *Dying for a Drink: What You Should Know About Alcoholism* (Dallas: Word Publishing, 1985). Dr. Spickard is a professor of medicine and the former director of the Vanderbilt Institute for Treatment of Alcoholics. An important Catholic book on alcoholism is Philip Maynard, *To Slake a Thirst: The Matt Talbot Way to Sobriety* (New York: Alba House, 2000). Matt Talbot was a Catholic alcoholic who experienced an extraordinary Christ-centered transformation. Matt Talbot was declared venerable by Pope Paul VI in 1975.

[19] Pope John Paul II, *The Role of the Christian Family in the Modern World* (*Familiaris Consortio*), 25.

[20] See George Barna, *Generation Next: What Every Parent and Youthworker Needs to Know About the Attitudes and Beliefs of Today's Youth* (Glendale, CA: Barna Research Group, 1995), p. 38.

[21] For Christian websites evaluating movies, go to: http://familylifecenter.net/article.asp?artId=309.

[22] Currently, the best DVD filtering option is ClearPlay filters and specially enabled DVD players. Visit http://www.clearplay.com/.

[23] For reviews of Internet filtering software, go to: http://internet-filter-review.toptenreviews.com/.

[24] Go to: http://dads.org/strugglewithporn.asp. The DVD, *Every Young Man's Battle*, is recommended for teenaged boys.

[25] www.dads.org.

[26] Barbara Hattemer and Robert Showers, *Don't Touch That Dial:*

The Impact of the Media on Children and the Family (Lafayatte, LA: Huntington House Publishers, 1993), p. 143.

[27] Cited from the True Lies website http://www.truelies.org/.

[28] According to a study by the National Center for Health Statistics, more than half of all teenagers have had oral sex. *The Washington Post*, "Study: Half of All Teens Have Had Oral Sex," September 16, 2005, page A07. Engaging in oral sex has spread to students at Catholic grade schools, middle schools, and especially at Catholic high schools and colleges. The same study reported that seventy percent of 18- and 19-year-olds have engaged in oral sex.

[29] See James Burnham and Stephen Wood, *Christian Fatherhood*, p. 127; John J. Nicola, *Diabolical Possession and Exorcism* (Rockford, IL: TAN Books, 1974), p. 151; Ralph Martin, *The Catholic Church at the End of an Age: What is the Spirit Saying?* (San Francisco: Ignatius, 1994), pp. 31-32; Stefano M. Paci, "Leo XIII's Diabolical Vision," *30 Days* (December, 1990), p. 52; *'Neath St. Michael's Shield* (Boston, MA: St. Paul Books, 1980), pp. 11-12, 24. For the full version of the St. Michael prayer http://dads.org/prayermichael.asp. In Revelation 20:1-3, 7-8 is a description of Satan's binding and being cast into the Abyss, and his subsequent loosing towards the end of the age.

Anne Catherine Emmerich experienced a vision parallel to Pope Leo XIII's: "In the centre of Hell I saw a dark and horrible-looking abyss, and into this Lucifer was cast, after being first strongly secured with chains; thick clouds of sulphurous black smoke arose from its fearful depths, and enveloped his frightful form ... I was likewise told, if I remember rightly, that he will be unchained for a time fifty or sixty years before the year of Christ 2000 ... but a certain number of demons are to be let loose much earlier than Lucifer, in order to tempt men. I should think that some must be loosened even in the present day [1823], and others will be set free in a short time." *The Dolorous Passion of Our LORD Jesus Christ* (Rockford, IL: TAN Publishers, 1983), p. 349.

[30] Catholics can begin investigating good homeschooling options by contacting Seton Home Study School (http://www.setonhome. org/), or the Mother of Divine Grace School (http://www.

motherofdivinegrace.org/). The Family Life Center also offers CDs introducing Catholic homeschooling (www.familylifecenter. net).

[31] *Sarasota Herald-Tribune*, "Study Shows Kids Schooled at Home Are Better Behaved," June 16, 1992, reporting on an unpublished doctoral dissertation for University of Florida's College of Education, "Comparison of Social Adjustment Between Home and Traditionally Schooled Students." Dr. Shyers is now a psychotherapist who is the Chairman of the Florida Board of Clinical Social Work, Marriage and Family Therapy, and Mental Health Counseling. Results of similar studies on homeschooling and socialization can be found at http://www.hslda.org/docs/ nche/000000/00000068.asp#7.

[32] The Home School Hall of Fame http://www.hslda.org/docs/ nche/000000/00000071.asp

[33] To learn how homeschoolers can earn athletic scholarships, see http://www.hslda.org/docs/nche/000002/00000217.asp.

[34] To read the entire CBS News article "Young Star Puts Motocross on Map," go to http://www.cbsnews.com/stories/2004/06/16/ eveningnews/main623560.shtml

[35] Of course, a part-time home-based business or job is a possibility for a homeschooling mother.

[36] *Catechism,* par. 2200.

[37] The words in bold in this chapter, such as, "heed," "listen," "obey," and "hear" are all derived from the same Hebrew word (*shama*).

[38] Cardinal Ratzinger at a Vatican press conference on Fatima, quoted in *Inside the Vatican*, May 2005, p. 87.

[39] *Emerging Trends*, Volume 21, No. 5 (May 1997), pp. 4-5, Princeton Religion Research Center.

[40] Some reputable Catholic psychologists include: Drs. Paul Vitz, William Bellet, Ray Guarendi, Joseph Nicolosi, and Richard Fitzgibbons, M.D. (psychiatrist). This list is not intended to be complete.

[41] *Catechism*, par. 123.

[42] *Catechism*, par. 121 and 122.

[43] *Catechism*, par. 122, quoting *Dei Verbum*, 15.

[44] Pope Pius XI, *On Christian Education* (*Divini Illius Magistri*), December 8, 1929, par 59.

[45] It should also be mentioned that the corporal punishment views of an individual saint raising children does not outweigh a papal encyclical.

[46] St. Thomas Aquinas' unique dignity was declared by Pope Leo XIII when he called him the "Angelic Doctor" and the "prince and master of all Scholastic doctors."

[47] St. Thomas Aquinas, *Summa Theologica*, Volume 3, Part II-II, Question 65. (Translated by Fathers of the English Dominican Province, Westminster, MD: Christian Classics, 1948).

[48] Pope Pius XII, *Dear Newlyweds: Pope Pius XII Speaks to Young Couples*, Selected and translated by James F. Murray, Jr. and Bianca M. Murray (New York, Farrar: Straus and Cudahy, 1961), pp. 185-186.

[49] Barbara and Timothy Friberg, *Friberg Analytical Greek Lexicon*, in *Bible Works* computer program, version 6.

[50] St. John Chrysostom, "Homily II on II Thessalonians," in vol. XIII of *The Nicene and Post-Nicene Fathers* (Grand Rapids, MI: Eerdmans, reprint May 1983). The works of St. John Chrysostom can also be accessed online at http://www.ccel.org/ccel/schaff/npnf113.html, p. 383.

[51] *Ibid*, pp. 383-384.

[52] Gerhard Kittle and Gerhard Friedrich, editors, translated by Geoffrey W. Bromiley Kittle, *Theological Dictionary of the New Testament* (abridged), (Grand Rapids, MI: Eerdmans, 1985), p. 756.

[53] Kittle and Friedrich, p. 757.

[54] St. John Chrysostom, "Homily XXI on Ephesians," in vol. XIII

of *The Nicene and Post-Nicene Fathers* (Grand Rapids, MI: Eerdmans, reprint May 1983), p. 157.

55 St. John Chrysostom, "Homily LIX on Matthew," in vol. X of *The Nicene and Post-Nicene Fathers* (Grand Rapids, MI: Eerdmans, reprint May 1983), p. 370.

56 *Catechism of the Council of Trent*, translated into English with notes by John A. McHugh and Charles J. Callan (Rockford, IL: TAN Books and Publishers, 1976), p. xxxvi.

57 *Catechism of the Council of Trent*, p. 419.

58 *Catechism of the Council of Trent*, p. 418.

59 *Dear Newlyweds*, p. 185.

60 *Dear Newlyweds*, p. 185.

61 See Leonard Sax, *Why Gender Matters: What Parents and Teachers Need to Know About the Emerging Science of Sex Differences* (New York: Doubleday, 2005). Christina Hoff Sommers, *The War Against Boys: How Misguided Feminism is Harming Our Young Men* (New York: Simon and Schuster, 2000).

62 Leonard Sax, *Why Gender Matters*, pp. 180-181.

63 1 Corinthians 13:12, 2 Corinthians 3:18, Matthew 5:8, 1 John 3:2. *Catechism*, par. 1028 and 1720.

64 Numbers 6:24-27: "'The LORD bless you and keep you: The LORD make his face to shine upon you, and be gracious to you: The LORD lift up his countenance upon you, and give you peace.' So shall they put my name upon the people of Israel, and I will bless them." Also see Psalm 67:1, 80:3, and Daniel 9:17.

65 Jeremiah 18:17, Isaiah 57:17, 2 Chronicles 30:9.

66 Richard W. Cross, "The Problem of Spanking: The Vexing Question of Childhood Discipline in the Development of Conscience" in *Defending the Family: A Sourcebook* (Steubenville, OH: The Catholic Social Science Press, 1999), pp. 195 – 233. Available online at http://catholiceducation.org/articles/parenting/pa0021.html.

[67] Stephen Wood, *The ABCs of Choosing a Good Husband* (Port Charlotte, FL: Family Life Center Publications, 2001), pp. 16-17.

[68] Bishop Bruskewitz said that this document contained, "bad advice, mistaken theology, erroneous science, and skewed sociology". He especially warns parents against the advice not to intervene. See his complete comments at http://www.christusrex.org/www1/mcitl/ezine.html.

[69] Joseph Nicolosi & Linda Ames Nicolosi, *A Parent's Guide to Preventing Homosexuality* (Downers Grove, IL: InterVarsity Press, 2002). "Homosexuality and Hope: Statement of The Catholic Medical Association", November 2000, http://www.narth.com/docs/hope.html.

[70] Joseph Nicolosi & Linda Ames Nicolosi, *A Parent's Guide to Preventing Homosexuality*, p. 31.

[71] I realize that there are many good exceptions, but they are still exceptions in today's effeminate Christian environments.

[72] The Pure Mind Scripture Memory Kits are available from the Family Life Center at: http://www.familylifecenter.net/cart/product_detail.cfm?ID=396. For a free downloadable Scripture memory program containing the same verses, go to: http://dads.org/article.asp?artId=319. My booklet, *Breaking Free*, has a brief comment after each of these recommended Scriptures to build understanding of what you are memorizing. http://www.familylifecenter.net/cart/product_detail.cfm?Id=587.

[73] See the "Saving Marriages" resources listed at http://familylifecenter.net.

[74] See Chapter One, "Attract a Man Who Will Love You as a Person," in *The ABCs of Choosing a Good Husband.*

[75] Wendy Shalit, *A Return to Modesty: Discovering The Lost Virtue* (New York: The Free Press, 1999). Shalit's book is not appropriate for younger girls, but her stories about her discovery that her friends' happiness seemed to coincide with their modesty and chastity can be conveyed by a father. Also see the story about John Blanchard meeting the girl with a rose in Grand Central Station in

my book, *The ABCs of Choosing a Good Husband*, pp. 11-14.

[76] *The Washington Times*, September 5, 2005, reporting on a survey by ACNielsen International Research, said that thousands of successful home-based businesses are established on eBay every year.

[77] Moving to a farm is an impossibility for most families, yet farm life remains one of the ideal environments in which to raise a family. The farm doesn't need to be your main source of income in order to create the family unity arising from farmwork. A small farm is still a possibility in our day. Visit www.dads.org for my article on "Farming and Family Life."

[78] The Pontifical Council for the Family, *The Truth and Meaning of Human Sexuality: Guidelines for Education within the Family* (Boston: Pauline Books and Media, 1995), section 86.

[79] Pope Leo XIII, *Freemasonry (Humanum Genus)*.

[80] *U.S. News and World Report*, September 13, 2004, pp. 47, 49 & 50, reporting on the survey, "Children, Media, and Consumer Culture" and the book, *Born to Buy* by Juliet Schor.

[81] Pope John Paul II, *Catechesis in Our Time* (*Catechesi Tradendae)*, 68.

[82] *USA Today*, August 18, 2005, citing a 1996 survey by the University of Maryland Center for Social Research.

[83] *AD 2000*, August 2000, p. 7.

[84] *Fidelity Magazine,* March 2004, p. 12.

[85] Thomas Karras, "The Truth About Men and the Church," Orthodox News Service, July 2, 2003 (http://www.orthodoxnews. netfirms.com/25/The%20Truth%20About%20Men%20&%20 Church.htm) reporting on a 1994 Swiss Study found in Volume 2 of *Population Studies* No. 31, (Volume 2 is entitled "The Demographic Characteristics of National Minorities in Certain European States," edited by Werner Haug and others, published by the Council of Europe Directorate General III, Social Cohesion, Strasbourg, Switzerland, January 2000).

[86] Thomas Karras, "The Truth About Men and the Church."

[87] Josh McDowell and Bob Hostetler, *Right from Wrong: What You Need to Know To Help Youth Make Right Choices* (Dallas: Word Publishing, 1994), p. 276.

[88] For suggestions for Catholic Scripture study go to: http://familylifecenter.net/article.asp?artId=287.

[89] Dietrich von Hildebrand, *The New Tower of Babel: Manifestations of Man's Escape from God* (Chicago: Franciscan Herald Press, 1977), p. 167.

[90] Dietrich von Hildebrand, *The New Tower of Babel: Manifestations of Man's Escape from God.* His entire chapter on "The Role of Reverence in Education" is invaluable, pp. 167-179.

[91] Mother Teresa, letter to Stephen Wood and all the St. Joseph's Covenant Keepers, July 1997. The complete letter is reproduced in *Christian Fatherhood*, p. 7.

[92] "Ten Benefits of Frequent Family Dinners," from The National Center on Addiction and Substance Abuse at Columbia University (CASA) http://casacolumbia.org

[93] This is a prayer that I composed for my own use. I've included it in case other fathers may want to use all, or portions, of it. Since it is a private prayer, it does not have official ecclesiastical approval.

LEGACY BOOK-ON-CD

Read by the author, this unabridged audio book makes for great drive-time listening for every dad.

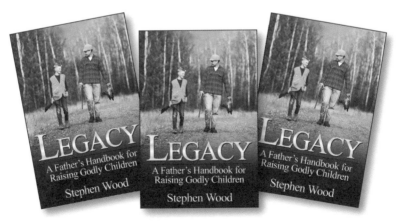

Call or visit our website to order additional copies of this groundbreaking book.

800.705.6131
www.dads.org

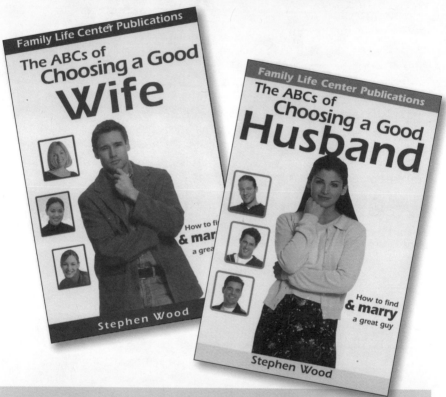

A WEBSITE JUST FOR DADS

www.dads.org

The official website for St. Joseph's Covenant Keepers

- Free newsletter for men
- Resources for fathering children and teens
- Tools for safe media in the family
- Dozens of articles relevant for fathers
- Prayer support
- Help for common family problems
- Info on men's conferences and small groups

FREE Dads e-Newsletter

Each issue features articles on faith, family, and fathering
that are designed to help you become the best husband
and dad you can be! Sign up online.

ABOUT THE AUTHOR

Stephen Wood has led youth, campus, and pro-life ministries. A graduate of Gordon-Conwell Theological Seminary, he served as an Evangelical pastor for a decade before entering the Catholic Church in 1990. Inspired by the family teaching of Pope John Paul II, he started the Family Life Center International in 1992. Stephen is also the founder of St. Joseph's Covenant Keepers, a worldwide movement that seeks to transform society through the transformation of fathers and families.

Utilizing his book *Christian Fatherhood*, CDs and DVDs, television, radio, newsletters, and conferences, Stephen has reached tens of thousands of men in the United States, Canada, and overseas with a message of Christian faith and responsibility. He is the host of the live *Faith and Family* broadcasts on EWTN worldwide radio, as well as the host of *The Carpenter's Shop*, a show for fathers on EWTN worldwide television.

A member of the American Counseling Association, Stephen is also a Certified Family Life Educator and a Christian Life Coach.

Stephen and Karen Wood have been married twenty-seven years and are the parents of eight children.